Robert Richardson

The Story of the Niger

A Record of Travel and Adventure from the Days of Mungo Park....

Robert Richardson

The Story of the Niger
A Record of Travel and Adventure from the Days of Mungo Park....

ISBN/EAN: 9783337242138

Printed in Europe, USA, Canada, Australia, Japan

Cover: Foto ©Andreas Hilbeck / pixelio.de

More available books at **www.hansebooks.com**

Story of the Niger

Ruins of the Cottage at Fowlshiels, near Selkirk, in which Mungo Park was born.

Thomas Nelson and Sons,
LONDON, EDINBURGH, AND NEW YORK.

STORY OF THE NIGER

*A Record of Travel and Adventure
From the Days of Mungo Park
To the Present Time.*

BY

Robert Richardson,

AUTHOR OF "ADVENTUROUS BOAT VOYAGES," "ALMOST A HERO,"
"RALPH'S YEAR IN RUSSIA,"
ETC ETC.

WITH 91 ILLUSTRATIONS

London:
T. NELSON AND SONS, PATERNOSTER ROW.
EDINBURGH; AND NEW YORK.

1888.

Preface.

This Story of the Niger is a rapid summary of facts. The material upon which the narrative is based is found scattered over many bulky volumes, such as few readers would have either the leisure or the inclination to attack. But it has been thought that, from the intrinsic interest of the story, a brief continuous narrative might prove acceptable to all who love a tale of travel and adventure. The story in these pages is essentially that told by the actors in the drama themselves, and is such as demanded no decoration at second hand. What has been aimed at was simply to collect all that was most striking and interesting, most pathetic or most humorous, and to weld the whole together in a consecutive and trustworthy narrative.

Attention may be called specially to the Sketch

Map of the Basins of the Senegal and Niger, showing Mungo Park's intended route on his second expedition to Central Africa, which is here reproduced in facsimile from the original drawing made by the traveller, and presented by him to his niece, Miss Jane Park.

R. R.

Contents.

I. AFRICAN DISCOVERY PREVIOUS TO PARK, ...	15
II. PARK'S FIRST JOURNEY, ...	22
III. PARK'S SECOND JOURNEY,	78
IV. CLAPPERTON AND THE LANDERS, ...	92
V. EXPLORATION OF THE NIGER AND BENUEH,	120
VI. CAPTAIN GALLIENI'S EXPEDITION TO THE UPPER NIGER,	154
VII. DR. BARTH'S TRAVELS, ...	267
VIII. MR. THOMPSON ON THE NIGER,	326

List of Illustrations.

MUNGO PARK SEEING THE MOSS IN THE DESERT,	*Frontispiece*
RUINS OF THE COTTAGE AT FOWLSHIELS, NEAR SELKIRK, IN WHICH MUNGO PARK WAS BORN,	*Vignette*
MAP OF CENTRAL AFRICA, SHOWING THE BASIN OF THE NIGER AND ADJACENT COUNTRIES,	xiv
MAP OF PARK'S TRAVELS IN AFRICA, WITH THE COURSE OF THE NIGER,	23
MUNGO PARK'S FIRST SIGHT OF THE NIGER,	43
TOWN HOUSE OF THE SOMONOS OF SEGO, ON THE NIGER,	47
THE NEGRO SONG,	51
A LION IN THE WAY,	59
MEAT-MARKET AT YAMINA, ON THE NIGER,	63
BAMBOO BRIDGE ACROSS THE BAFING,	75
FACSIMILE OF SKETCH MAP OF MUNGO PARK'S INTENDED ROUTE IN HIS SECOND EXPEDITION TO THE NIGER.—*From a Drawing by himself,*	87
RIVER SCENE IN WESTERN AFRICA,	107
KING OBIE'S VISIT TO THE "ALBURKAH,"	123
FRENCH EXPEDITION AGAINST THE TOUCOULEURS,	159
GALLIENI'S EXPEDITION ON THE SENEGAL BETWEEN MATAM AND BAKEL,	165
FIRE ON THE LEFT BANK OF THE BAKHOY, NEAR DEMBA-DIOUBE,	179
VILLAGE OF SOLINTA, ON THE BAKHOY,	183
FOREST NEAR THE BILY FALLS, ON THE BAKHOY,	191
THE REFRACTORY ASS-DRIVERS,	195
IMPROVISED BRIDGE OVER THE KEGNEKO,	201

LIST OF ILLUSTRATIONS.

REVIEW ON THE PLAINS OF KITA TO CELEBRATE THE TREATY OF PROTECTORATE WITH FRANCE,	207
CROSSING THE BANDINGHO,	211
RETREAT OF GALLIENI'S EXPEDITION FROM DIO,	219
TORNADO IN THE BIRGO COUNTRY,	231
MARKET AT SOKOTO,	275
SONGHAY VILLAGE,	283
TIMBUCTOO,	301
ENCAMPMENT OF SHEIK EL BAKAY,	307
A NUPE VILLAGE,	339
FILLANI NOBLEMAN AND ATTENDANTS,	343
VIEW IN SOKOTO,	347

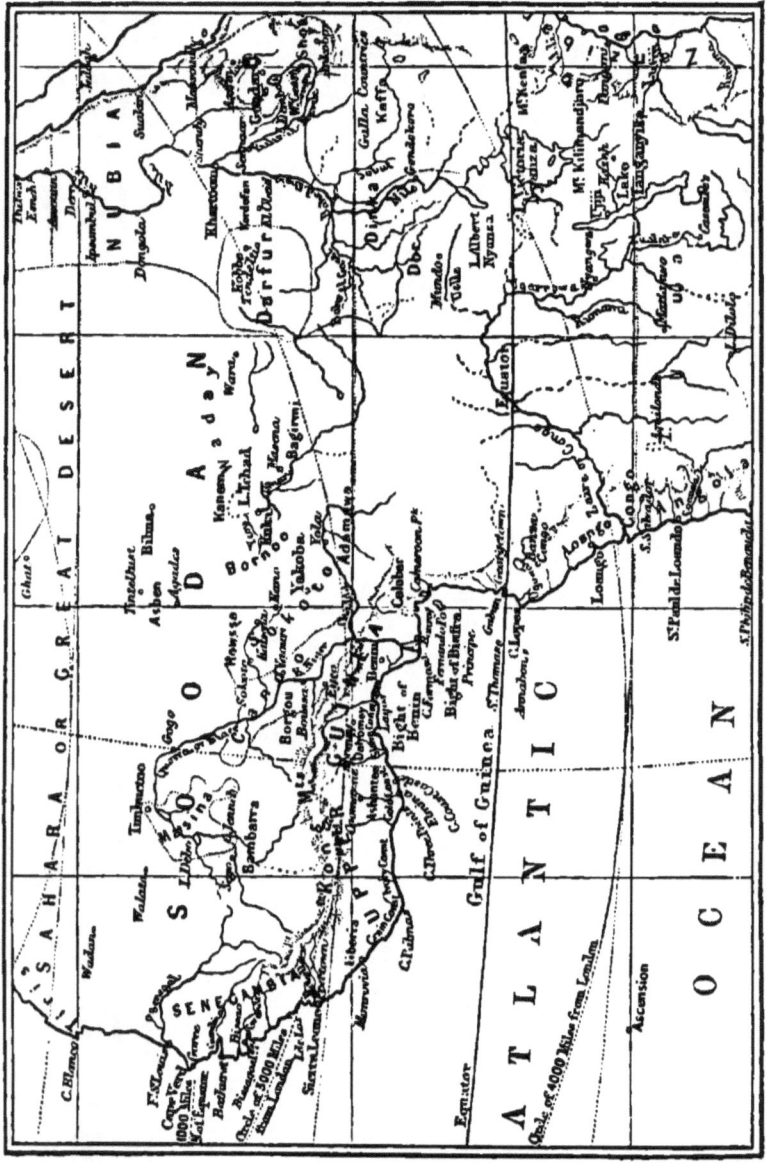

MAP OF CENTRAL AFRICA, SHOWING THE BASIN OF THE NIGER AND ADJACENT COUNTRIES.

STORY OF THE NIGER.

CHAPTER I.

AFRICAN DISCOVERY PREVIOUS TO PARK.

From very early times down to the present day Africa has exercised a fascination for the traveller: no weaker word will so well serve to express the truth. At this moment no other land seems to possess such a spell for the discoverer—not even the regions of the North Pole. The two geographical secrets which our modern explorers, land and maritime, most covet, are probably the discovery of the remaining sources of the Nile and the discovery of the North Pole.

To the ancients, Africa was a land of mystery and marvel; and though every year now sees some new region in its vast territory opened up and reclaimed from darkness, it is to a large extent a land of mystery and marvel still. It still offers to the explorer an unrivalled field for discovery and adventure.

The nations of antiquity were, however, perfectly well acquainted with the northern portions of Africa—those bordering on the Mediterranean Sea, and including Carthage and Egypt. It was in respect to the regions beyond this circuit that their knowledge was vague and conflicting. South of the countries skirting the sea-board extended the immeasurable tract of desert now known as the Great Sahara, whose vastness and appalling desolation were for long sufficient to daunt the most adventurous spirits, checking the advance alike of the conqueror and the traveller.

The interest attached to early African discovery may be said to centre in the river Niger. When the attention of modern European nations began to be turned towards Africa as a land offering rich opportunities for the acquisition of territory, and the increase of national wealth and power, it was quickly seen that the Niger formed the natural highway to the heart of the country; and to hold the secret of the mighty river, to trace and follow its course throughout its whole vast extent, became the chief object of ambition among the discoverers of many different lands.

Among the earliest historical references—probably *the* earliest reference—to what modern geographers have supposed to be the Niger, is to be found in an account given by Herodotus of a journey made by five young Nasamones of noble birth and ardent spirit, who may be regarded as having formed the first Geographical Association. After a long and adventurous journey, the travellers came upon a great river flowing from west to east, on whose banks dwelt a nation of small black men. This river Herodotus without hesitation declared to be the Nile. That it was not the Nile is certain; and even that it was the Niger is a disputed point among those who have most closely considered the question. It has been contended by some writers that the young Nasamones, by following the course described by their historian, could never have reached the Quorra or Niger; while others maintain that such a goal to their journey was quite possible, and that the city which the travellers found on the banks of the river, peopled by a diminutive race of black men, was no other than Timbuctoo.

Mention is made of the Niger by both Strabo and Pliny, the former briefly, the latter at great length. Pliny adopts the idea of Herodotus that the Niger was one and the same river with the Nile; but when Ptolemy comes to treat the subject he directly controverts this theory, though, from lack of accurate knowledge, he offers nothing in its place save vague surmise.

We learn a good deal of the geography of Africa from Arabian writers, but very little that is either accurate or even suggestive in regard to the river Niger. The Arabs at one time exercised a great influence over Africa—planted colonies, built cities, carried on an extensive commerce with the natives in gold and slaves, and finally established themselves as the dominant power in the land. The most famous among Arabian travellers was Ibu Batutu, a Mohammedan gentleman distinguished by his learning and accomplishments, who lived in the fourteenth century. In the course of his travels, Ibu Batutu undoubtedly beheld the Niger, but made the same mistake in regard to it as had been made by older writers, supposing it to be identical with the Nile.

The next traveller who contributed anything noteworthy to our knowledge of Africa was the geographer Leo, a native of Granada, who, for his explorations in the African continent, received the cognomen of Africanus. He, too, elaborated a theory in regard to the Niger, affirming that it had its source in a lake lying to the south of Bornou.

While Portugal was in the zenith of her power, and her ships were supreme upon the seas, she directed her energies towards Africa with a view to colonization and national aggrandizement. Portuguese navigators made important discoveries along the western shores of the continent, opening up to commerce and the world the mouths of three several rivers—the Senegal, the Gambia, and the Rio Grande—all of which they believed to be the channels by which the Niger emptied itself into the Atlantic. The power and influence of Portugal, both on land and sea, waned until the nation ceased to be a factor in the councils of Europe. But after a long period of inglorious torpor in the direction of discovery and scientific enterprise, Portugal is again showing signs of coming to the front, if we may take as evidence the recent spirited and wonderful journey of Major Serpo Pinta across Africa.

From this brief survey of early African discovery it will be seen that the river Niger, though it was made the focus of exploration, for a long period baffled the attempts of travellers to determine accurately either its source or its course. It was reserved for England to pierce and dissipate the thick cloud of obscurity which veiled the great river. Yet this was not accomplished immediately, nor without sacrifice.

An association was formed in England in 1788, which took the title of the African Association. As its name suggests, the object of the association was to stimulate and encourage African discovery. The endeavours of the committee to find persons willing and competent to attempt the arduous task of penetrating into the interior of Africa met with a quick response, the first volunteer for the required work being Mr. Ledyard. The chief qualifications which this gentleman possessed for the enterprise, besides dauntless courage and great ardour, were his having been a comrade of the illustrious Cook in his voyage round the world, and his having spent many years of adventurous life among the North American Indians. Mr. Ledyard's career in Africa was a sadly brief one. While at Cairo, whence his expedition was to set out, he was laid low by fever, induced, there can be little doubt, by the fretting of his eager and impetuous spirit at some hindrance in the starting of his caravan. Hasty and injudicious treatment of himself completed what anxiety and vexation had begun; and thus the first envoy of the African Association brought to an untimely close an enterprise which, had intrepidity and enthusiasm been all that was required, might have had a brilliant and important issue.

The next traveller employed by the Association was Mr. Lucas. He was unfortunate in the timing of his journey, for the regions of Africa through which he endeavoured to pass were in a disturbed and dangerous state, owing to a rebellion among the Moors. Neither camels nor guides could be procured, and at last the traveller was obliged to abandon his enterprise. Nevertheless Mr. Lucas succeeded in collecting various notes relative to the country contiguous to Tripoli, which added something to the general knowledge of Africa.

It will be observed that these two attempts to advance into the interior of Africa were land expeditions. The next undertaken was so far of the same character, but the start was from an entirely different point. Major

Houghton, the third adventurer in the field of African exploration, chose the route by the river Gambia, believing that he would thereby most surely and quickly reach the Niger. Few episodes in the record of African adventure are more pitiable than the fate of this gallant and ardent gentleman. He reached in safety Ferbanna, on the Falemé, where he was welcomed with every hospitality by the king, who forwarded him on his journey by all the means in his power. The next and last personal communication from Major Houghton told of his being in good health and spirits; but shortly thereafter the report came of his death—a report which was subsequently confirmed in every essential by Park. Plundered of everything he possessed, and left to wander without food and clothing in the heart of the desert, the ill-fated traveller perished of starvation, exposure, and fatigue.

CHAPTER II.

PARK'S FIRST JOURNEY.

WE now arrive at a very important stage in the history of African discovery — that marked by the appearance of Mungo Park. Park's success as a discoverer having so greatly exceeded that of any previous traveller, it is fitting that we should place before the reader a few particulars regarding his early life, before proceeding to give an epitome of his two great journeys.

Mungo Park's birth-place was Fowlshiels, near Selkirk, where he first saw the light in September 1771. The elder Park was a well-to-do farmer, who had so strong an infusion of the ambition common among Scottish parents of giving their children the best education in their power, that he engaged a tutor for his boys and girls—a rare proceeding on the part of a farmer in those days. Young Mungo Park subsequently attended a school in Selkirk, where he does not appear to have displayed more than an average degree of ability in his studies. He was fond of all

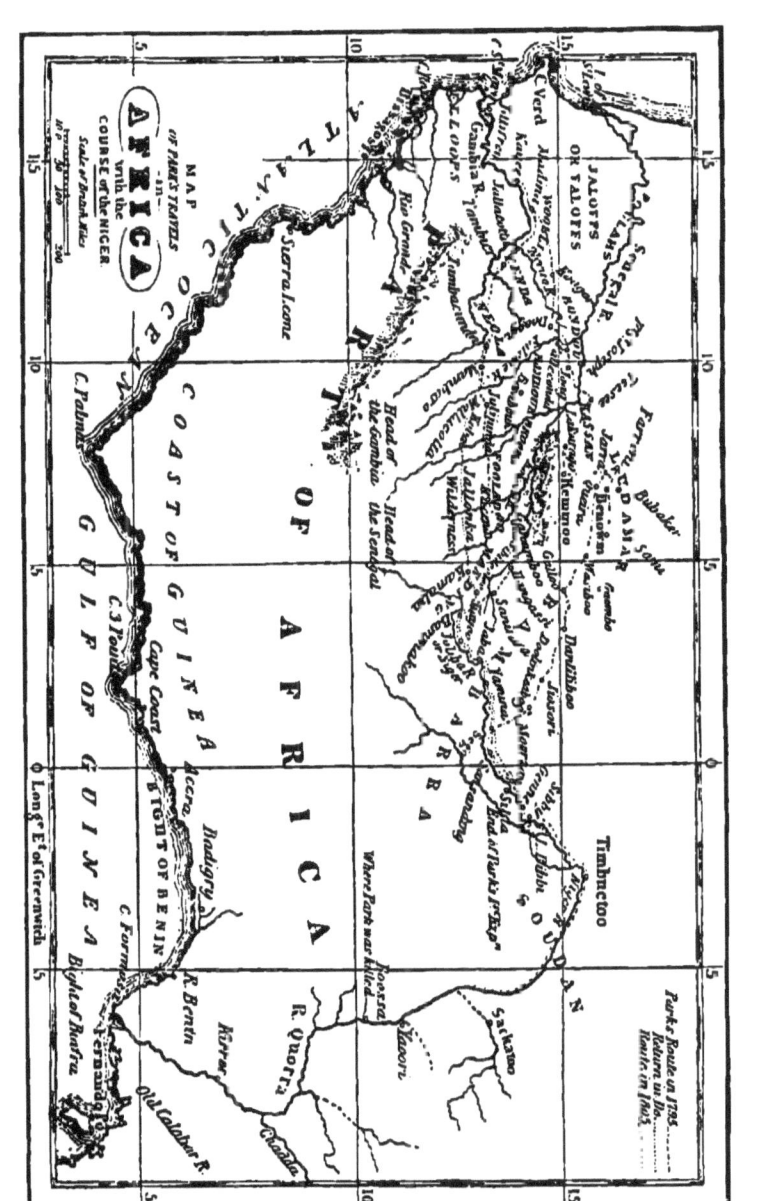

kinds of reading, however, and was generally of a thoughtful temperament. It is related of the boy that old romances and the stirring Border ballads were among his favourite reading, which would seem to indicate that beneath the quiet reserve of his outward bearing there smouldered no little imagination and enthusiasm.

It was the desire of his parents that young Mungo should study for the ministry, but the lad's own inclinations were not in this direction. He wished to follow the medical profession, and was accordingly apprenticed to a surgeon in Selkirk. In the year 1789 he began to attend the medical lectures at the Edinburgh University, and finished the usual three years' course. His favourite study at this time, and indeed always, was botany.

In 1792 Park sailed for Sumatra, as assistant surgeon on board the East Indiaman *Worcester*, returning to England after a year's absence. The desire of the African Association to find some individual qualified and ready to prosecute still further the work of exploration in Africa, and to endeavour to finish what Major Houghton and his predecessors had little more than begun, roused the ambition and enthusiasm of Park, and he offered his services to the Association. The committee deemed Mr. Park's qualifications for his task fully sufficient, his services were accepted, and preparations were begun for his departure for

Africa. Nearly two years elapsed, however, before he was ready to start.

Park sailed from Portsmouth on the 22nd of May 1795, and disembarked in Africa at Jillifree, a town on the Gambia. On the 5th July he reached Pisania, where he was warmly welcomed by Dr. Laidley. During a residence of five months with his hospitable host, Park attained to considerable proficiency in the Mandingo language; while at the same time he was active in studying the customs and character of the natives and the natural features of the country—a pursuit which even an attack of fever only partially interrupted. He describes the Gambia at this stage of its course as deep and muddy, its shores hidden by thickets of mangrove, the stream itself being full of fish of strange and unknown varieties, and higher up of hippopotami and alligators.

Mr. Park took leave of Dr. Laidley early in December 1795. His companions were three in number—a man, a boy, and a horse. The first was a native named Johnson, who spoke both English and Mandingo; the second a negro lad, Demba, who was also acquainted with several languages besides his own; while the horse was a small but wiry animal, of much spirit and hardihood. Johnson and Demba had also an ass each, which carried both their masters and the packs.

On December the 5th the little party of travellers

reached Medina, a town containing some one thousand houses, and the capital of the kingdom of Wooli. King Jatta, the ruling sovereign of Wooli, was the king who had so hospitably received Major Houghton during his sojourn in his dominions; and he now manifested the same disposition to befriend and assist Mr. Park. Nevertheless he thought it incumbent on him to try to dissuade the traveller from his journey, assuring him that the same fate which befell Major Houghton awaited every white man who should endeavour to pass through the countries east of Wooli. Mr. Park thanked the king for his kindly and well-meant advice, but said that he must at all hazards complete the task he had begun.

On the 8th the travellers reached Kolor, a town of some size, where Mr. Park first made the acquaintance of that curious African deity or demon—whichever it may be regarded as—*Mumbo Jumbo*. He beheld, suspended from the bough of a tree, a sort of masquerade suit made of bark, and this, he was informed, belonged to Mumbo Jumbo. A Kafir may marry as many wives as he pleases, or can afford to add to his household. One result of this system of polygamy, as it obtains among the Mandingoes, is that the wives occasionally fall out. When these intestine wars wax so fierce that the authority of the husband is set at defiance, the aid of Mumbo Jumbo is invoked, and seldom, it would appear, without the desired effect.

"This strange minister of justice," writes Mr. Park, "(who is supposed to be either the husband himself or some person instructed by him), disguised in the dress that has been mentioned, and armed with the rod of public authority, announces his coming by loud and dismal screams in the woods near the town. He begins the pantomime at the approach of night; and as soon as it is dark he enters the town and proceeds to the bentang, at which all the inhabitants immediately assemble." It will thus be seen that Mumbo Jumbo is the great bugbear or "Bogey" of Mandingo Kafir wives.

At Koojar, the frontier town of the kingdom of Bondou, our traveller was invited to witness a *neobering* or wrestling-match. The antagonists, athletic young men fired with emulation, stripped naked, save for a short pair of drawers, and with their limbs well lubricated with *shea* butter; like the competitors in the ancient classic games, approached each other on all fours. After some little feinting and warding the rivals closed, and then began a display of agility and strength which Mr. Park believed few English athletes would have been able to match. The combatants were stimulated in their contest by the music of a drum, to whose rude strains they even, in some degree, timed their movements.

On the morning of the 12th the travellers entered the wilderness that stretches between the kingdoms of Wooli and Bondou. At noon they found themselves beneath a large tree, the odd appearance of which could not fail to strike Mr. Park. The tree was called by the natives *Neema Taba*. Its branches were ornamented with a ragged drapery of scraps and patches of cloth which various travellers had fastened to them—at first, Mr. Park suggests, to indicate that water was to be found close at hand; and the custom having in time come to be regarded as a sort of religious rite, at length no wayfarer cared to pass without hanging up something.

Mr. Park's next halting-place was Tallika, the chief town in the Bondou territory, the inhabitants of which seemed to do a brisk commerce in supplying passing caravans with provisions, and also in ivory—two sources of wealth which enabled them to live in comfortable estate.

The travellers quitted Tallika on December 14th, but had ridden only a short distance when the harmony of the little company—which, it must be stated, was at this time increased by a party of Serawoollies—was interrupted by a fierce quarrel between two of the number. These breakers of the peace indulged in some very unflattering epithets towards each other; which causes Mr. Park to relate, as a circumstance worthy of note, that a blow is a much lighter insult to an African than a slighting word spoken of his relatives. "Strike me, but do not curse my mother," is an expression frequently heard even from the lips of slaves. Mr. Park took prompt measures to put an end to this unseemly quarrel between his fellow-travellers, by plainly informing the one who was manifestly in the wrong, that if he attempted to draw his cutlass again, he should regard him as a robber and shoot him on the spot—a threat which had all the desired effect. The above is an example of the prompt and fearless measures which Mr. Park could command whenever any crisis called for such—a quality all the more remarkable in one naturally disposed to be propitiatory, where propitiatory action would by any means serve his end.

On the 21st Mr. Park arrived at Fatteconda, the chief town in Bondou, where he was quickly presented to the king, Almami. The traveller approached the presence of this personage with some feeling of doubt, for he had heard that Almami's conduct towards Major Houghton was marked by great unkindness. Mr. Park therefore took the precaution of bringing with him gifts of some value. The king received the presents more graciously than the giver had hoped for, and then, after some long and circumlocutory praise of white men in general, their riches and their generosity, descended to particulars by passing a warm eulogium on Mr. Park's coat—a blue one, gay with yellow buttons — and finally wound up his speech in the manner that the traveller probably anticipated, by begging him to present him with the garment. Though the coat was the only good one in Mr. Park's possession, he deemed it politic to consent to the king's request, knowing that with an African prince a request is usually synonymous with a command. The traveller's mortification in this instance must have been all the greater from the circumstance that he had put on his new blue coat in the fond expectation that his back was the safest place for it—a process of reasoning altogether too simple for the occasion, as the event proved.

King Almami, however, so far reimbursed Mr. Park for the loss of his coat as to supply him with plenty of provisions, and subsequently—as a mark of special favour probably—introduced him to the ladies of his household, who had expressed a wish to see the stranger. This interview with King Almami's wives formed one of the funniest episodes in Park's travels.

These were about a dozen in number, for the most part of comely aspect and lively demeanour. Two features in the traveller's appearance especially surprised and amused them—the whiteness of his complexion, and the prominence of his nose. He had been washed in milk when a child, they insisted, and had thus become so white, while his nose had attained its present unnatural and preposterous shape by dint of daily pinching. Mr. Park met the badinage of the dusky beauties in a like light and lively vein, indulging in a liberal strain of compliment on the good looks of African ladies. His entertainers replied that *honey-mouth*, their expressive phrase for flattery, was but lightly regarded in Bondou. Nevertheless they did not seem altogether indifferent to the white man's approval, one proof of which may have been the little present—a jar of honey and some fish—which they afterwards sent to his hut.

Park quitted Fatteconda on the 23rd, and presently reached Joag, in the kingdom of Kagaaga, the inhabitants of which are called Serawoollies, a people who show a marked capacity for business, are fairly honest and straightforward in their dealings, and many of whom attain to comparative wealth from the sale of gold, salt, and cotton. Our traveller was not well treated by the Serawoollies, being robbed of his money by a party of horsemen, who pretended that he had contravened the laws of the country by entering it without paying duty. As an offset to this indignity, however, he met with unexpected kindness at the hands of an old woman, who beholding him sitting, disconsolate and hungry-looking, beneath a *bentang* tree, asked him if he had had his dinner. On Park's replying in the negative, and recounting the circumstances of his robbery, the old woman, placing on the ground the basket she had been carrying on her head, took from it some handfuls of nuts, and, with a look of much solicitude and pity, presented them to the white man. This was the first of many similar instances of spontaneous and unlooked-for kindness which Park experienced from the rude and untutored peoples among whom his journey led him, and it will be seen, as the narrative proceeds, how, in his sorest straits, he was especially indebted to women for succour and solace.

Park's next important halting-place was Kocniakari in the kingdom of Kasson, where he was well received by the king, Demba Sego Jalla, a favourable specimen of a native prince, whose prowess in war and clemency in peace had secured the sincere attachment of his people. Demba Sego Jalla had seen Major Houghton, and had made him a present of a white horse. He knew that the traveller had been killed by the Moors, but could not supply Mr. Park with the particulars of his death. Park was furnished by the king with two guides to conduct him to Kaarta, the capital of which, Kemmoo, he presently reached. Towards sunset of the same day he had an audience of the king (Daisey Koorabani) who received the white man seated simply on a bank of earth, which, covered with a leopard-skin, formed the royal throne. King Daisey was surrounded by a large body of guards and attendants, who preserved excellent order; but save for the elevation of his seat and the leopard-skin, there was nothing about the king to distinguish him from the rest of his court.

When Park had explained to King Daisey the circumstances and object of his journey, and asked his aid in forwarding him on his way, the latter listened to the traveller with attention, but replied that he would be unable to render him much assistance. There was feud between the people of Kaarta and of Bambarra, the adjoining kingdom; and hence it was impossible that the king of the former country could at present enter into friendly communication with one who was his enemy. King Daisey strongly recommended Mr. Park to return by the way he had come; but as the traveller expressed a firm determination not to do this, the king advised, as the next best course to adopt, that Park should proceed to Bambarra by a circuitous route through the Moorish territory of Ludamar. It was identically the same path which led Major Houghton to his death; but as he had no other choice, Park determined to follow it also, and on February the 13th set out from Kemmoo, accompanied by three of King Daisey's sons.

Shortly before entering Jarra, the frontier town of Ludamar, Park witnessed an episode of curious and painful interest. A native herdsman had been wounded by a Moorish robber, and was being slowly led home, supported on his horse by a number of comrades. In front of the little *cortége* walked the young man's mother, wild with grief, clapping with her hands, and singing the praises of her son—his virtues, gifts, and graces. "Ee maffo fonio!" (He never told a lie.) "Ee maffo fonio; abada" (He never told a lie; no, never!), she cried. The wounded youth was carried into her hut and placed upon a mat—a crowd of his friends gathering around the white, and bewailing the mishap with pitiable howling and moaning.

Mr. Park being requested to examine the young man's wound, did so, and found that the bone of the leg had sustained a serious fracture, which would necessitate the amputation of the limb, if there was to be any hope of saving the lad's life. This the boy's relatives and friends would not hear of, regarding it as an act of unheard-of cruelty; and the sufferer died the same evening.

On the 18th Park and his companions passed the village of Simbing, a place which must have had painful associations for the traveller; for it was from here that his gallant predecessor, Major Houghton, dated his last letter—written in pencil—to Dr. Laidley. Here Mr. Park heard the full particulars of Major Houghton's death (a brief account of which has already been given), and was shown from a distance the very spot where the traveller's body had been left a prey to the vulture and the jackal.

On his arrival at Jarra—a considerable town situated among rocky hills, substantially built of stone and clay, and inhabited by negroes subject to the

Moors—Park sent forward to Ali, the ruling chief of Ludamar, a propitiatory present consisting of cotton clothing. At Deena, the next large town at which the traveller halted, he had his first experience of the inhospitable and insulting treatment of which he was to have only too many examples during his sojourn among the Moors.

A crowd collected about the hut in which he was lodging, and forthwith began to yell, hiss, and abuse the unfortunate white man by every means they could devise, even to the length of spitting in his face. As a last method of rousing and if possible enraging their victim, they reviled him for being a Christian, and finally proceeded to strip him of everything of value which he possessed.

Proceeding still patiently on his journey, Park next passed through Sampaka and Samee, the latter a negro village, where he once more met with the hospitable entertainment which he so often received at the hands of the negroes, and which so agreeably contrasted with his treatment by the Moors. The *dooty*, or chief man of Samee, killed two fat sheep in the white man's honour, and liberally feasted him and his companions.

Refreshed in body and cheered in spirit by the timely and gentle ministrations of these simple people, Mr. Park was indulging the hope that he had nothing further to fear from the Moors, and was already dreaming of a successful and glorious issue to his journey, when hopes and dreams were alike rudely dispelled by the sudden appearance at the door of his hut of a party of Moors, who came to convey the white man to Ali's camp at Benowm. Park narrates that he was struck speechless with surprise and fear at the sight of these men—a condition of mind that was little allayed by their declaration that he had nothing to dread, and that their visit had been instigated chiefly by the desire of Queen Fatima, Ali's wife, to make acquaintance with the white man.

On March 12th, Park and his escort reached Benowm, which was little else than a collection of mean-looking tents, confusedly scattered over a large area, and among which herds of cattle, camels, and goats roamed at will. As the party entered the camp, Park, being exceedingly thirsty, endeavoured to obtain a little water. He was at length successful. But immediately the people at the wells beheld the white man, they flung down their water-pitchers; men, women, and children came running towards him; and Mr. Park presently found himself surrounded by so great a crowd that he was unable to move this way or that. Forthwith began a process of petty annoyance of the stranger: one pulled off his hat; others tugged at his coat; others insisted on examining his waistcoat buttons; and another, with significant threats, made him repeat after him the words, " Illa la el Allah,

Mahomet rasowl alabi" (There is but one God, and Mohammed is his prophet).

When the traveller was at length brought before Ali, he found that prince seated on a leather cushion, engaged in trimming his moustache, while a female slave held up a looking-glass before him. The king was an elderly man, with a flowing white beard, and a not very pleasant type of countenance, by reason of its sullen and angry expression. After looking fixedly at the stranger, he asked him if he could speak Arabic; and on Park's replying that he could not, he seemed greatly surprised, and resumed his former silence.

The ladies of the court, however, showed much greater inquisitiveness—putting innumerable questions to the white man; minutely examining his clothes; making him unbutton his vest, that they might see the whiteness of his skin; and, finally, counting his fingers and toes, in doubt, presumably, whether he had the same number as themselves.

At sunrise next day, Ali visited the traveller in his tent, to inform him that a hut had been made ready for him. Mr. Park found his new lodging cool and comfortable enough; but he had barely taken possession of it when he was once more assailed by a crowd of Moors, and the persecution of the hapless white man was renewed with greater persistence than ever. All that day, from noon till night, he was occupied in a series of dressings and undressings for the satisfaction and amusement of his visitors, being supported under this disagreeable and trying ordeal only by a slight supper of *kouskous* and salt and water, the only meal that was provided him during the day. The traveller had a comparatively quiet night's rest; but with daybreak began the same round of indignity and annoyance. "It is impossible," Mr. Park writes, "to describe the behaviour of a people who study mischief as a science, and exult in the miseries and misfortunes of their fellow-creatures."

In devising methods of persecuting their helpless victim, the Moors certainly displayed an ingenuity worthy of a better cause. The means they discovered and devised of rendering Mr. Park's life miserable were innumerable. No one was so degraded in this barbarous society but he might bait, bully, and insult the white man with impunity.

His captors seemed to think, or at least pretended to, that the white man was a master of all trades; for at one time he was bidden to perform the duties of a gunsmith, and mend a gun for one of the king's sons, and at another time those of a barber. He was not, however, asked a second time to fill the latter office, for on his first occasion of doing so he managed to give the person being operated on (the boy-prince of Ludamar) an unmistakable proof of his being a novice in the craft—namely, a cut on the side of the head; whereat the king, concluding that the head of his son and heir was in the wrong place, brought Mr. Park's performance to an abrupt conclusion.

An object of special curiosity, and presently of superstitious awe to the Moors, was the traveller's pocket-compass. Ali himself was most anxious to have the mystery of the needle explained to him—why it always pointed to the north, to the Great Desert. Unable to devise any other answer that would have met the case, Mr. Park told the king that his mother dwelt beyond the Sahara Desert, and that as long as she lived the needle of the compass would point towards her home, thus serving as a guide to direct him to her; and that when she died it would point to her grave—a harmless fabrication which got the traveller out of his difficulty, for it would have been futile to have attempted any scientific explanation of the matter. The king now regarded the compass with added astonishment and awe, and after turning it this way and that in his hands, following the motions of the needle with a face of silent wonder, he returned the little instrument to its owner, with every sign of fear at retaining any longer in his keeping so magical and potent a charm.

Almost every day brought the captive white man new hardships and annoyances, and thus a whole month dragged wearily along. Every sunset he eagerly welcomed the night, for then only was there respite for him from the persecutions of his oppressors.

He was insufficiently fed, and on the coarsest fare—a bowl of kouskous with a little salt and water constituting his single daily meal. But he suffered most of all from thirst, for it was the dry season, and the heat was intense.

One evening, having in vain tried to procure a drink in the camp, Park, feverish from thirst, wandered out into the night, if by any chance he might obtain a draught of water at the wells, which were about half a mile distant from the town. Having accosted an old man who was busy drawing water, and requested that he might be allowed to drink, the man was at first about to hand him his bucket, when, suddenly calling to mind that he was a Christian, he emptied the contents of the bucket into a common cow-trough, and bade the white man drink from it. It was not a time to regard niceties, and the fever-parched white man was fain to thrust his head between those of two cows, and take a long and deep draught from the rude trough.

All this time Park had seen nothing of Queen Fatima, who was the ostensible cause of his being brought to Benowm and detained so long there; but at last he had an interview with the Moorish princess, at her residence in Bubaker. She was a woman of enormous size—corpulence being regarded among the Moors as the most distinguished mark of female beauty—with long black hair. At first she showed some signs of being scandalized at the close proximity of a Christian, but presently received Mr. Park graciously enough, questioned him about his native land, and finally dismissed him with a present of a bowl of milk.

Again: it is worthy of being noted, that even among the Moors, whose treatment of Park was characterized by universal harshness and oppression, the only real kindness that he received was from a woman, Fatima continuing to befriend him to the end. The queen persuaded her husband to allow the traveller to return with him to Jarra, Mr. Park being at this time, it will be remembered, at Bubaker.

After a few days' stay at Jarra, Ali returned to Bubaker to celebrate an approaching feast, and Mr. Park was left to await the king's return. On the 14th of June, news was brought to Jarra that King Daisey, with whom Ali was at war, was about to attack the camp. On the 26th, information arrived that Daisey had captured Simbing, and would be in Jarra immediately. Whereupon one-half of the inhabitants abandoned the town, and set out for Bambarra.

In the general confusion which now ensued in Jarra, Park resolved to attempt his escape. Mounting his horse, and throwing a bag of corn across his saddle, he joined the retreating crowd of townspeople, and mingled in the hurrying throng of men, women, and

MUNGO PARK'S FIRST SIGHT OF THE NIGER.

children, cattle, sheep, and goats. The panic-stricken band of refugees, abandoning their homes and possessions, presented a sad and pitiful sight, which even Mr. Park, much as he had suffered at the hands of the Moors, could not help compassionating.

A crisis had arrived in Park's life. Now, if ever, an opportunity for escape from the Moors seemed to present itself. "I was again," he writes, "either to taste the blessings of freedom or languish out my days in captivity." Taking with him a small bundle, and bidding farewell to the negro Johnson, who had been so long his faithful companion, he escaped by night while his guards were asleep. He had placed some distance between himself and his captors, and had begun to indulge a feeling of security, when he heard a hallooing behind him: three horsemen galloped up, caught hold of his horse, and told him he must return with them to Ali.

This unlooked-for downfall of all his hopes affected Park with the indifference and apathy of despair. But things were not so bad as they at first seemed. The three men had really no authority from Ali to apprehend Mr. Park, and had followed him merely with the object of plunder. Having accomplished their purpose, they suffered the traveller to go free; and Mr. Park, his spirits again rising at having escaped with his life, turned his face eastward, and presently entered the forest.

Great as was Mr. Park's joy in the feeling of being once more a free man, he soon became alive to the gravity of his situation. He was without food and without water, faint from hunger and parched with thirst, while his horse was in much the same condition, becoming presently too weak to support his rider's weight.

Park now sank into a state of such extreme prostration that his consciousness for a time left him, and he fell into a faint. By-and-by, however, he recovered, and determining to make one more effort for his life, pushed wearily but patiently on, in the hope of reaching some pool of water—his only chance of restoring his exhausted energies. Presently he beheld a flash of lightning, followed by a second and a third; the forest began to shake in the rising wind, and soon a few heavy rain-drops pattered down on the traveller. For upwards of an hour rain fell fast, and Mr. Park succeeded in quenching his thirst by soaking his clothes and then sucking them dry.

The traveller pushed on, but it was not long ere he was again suffering from thirst. This time he was relieved more sufficiently. He heard a loud croaking of frogs, a "heavenly sound" to his ears, and shortly thereafter reached a shallow muddy pool, at which both himself and his horse fully quenched their thirst. On the same day he reached Shrilla, a Foulah village, where he sought entertainment at the house of the

TOWN HOUSE OF THE SOMONOS OF SEGO, ON THE NIGER.

Page 50.

dooty, but was inhospitably turned from the door. At some little distance, spinning cotton, sat an old woman at the entrance of her hut. This kind old creature led the hungry and tired traveller into her cabin, set food before him, and brought corn for his horse; in return for which good offices Mr. Park made her accept one of his handkerchiefs.

On July the 15th our traveller halted at Wawra, a small negro town, where, being greatly fatigued, he rested a while. Resuming his journey, he passed through several other negro towns and villages, travelling now for the most part on foot, for his horse had become so weak that his master forbore making any attempt to ride him.

As Mr. Park approached the town of Sego, visions of the Niger so filled his thoughts and his imagination that they prevented him from sleeping. It was evening as he drew near the town, when, gazing about him to catch sight of the river, he heard one of his companions, who consisted of Kaartan natives, call out, "Geo affilli!" (See the water!) And directing his gaze forward, he beheld, with satisfaction and joy that may be imagined, the great object of his mission—"the long-sought-for, majestic Niger, glittering to the morning sun, as broad as the Thames at Westminster, and flowing slowly *to the eastward*." The discoverer of the great river, with mingled emotions of elation and thankfulness, hurried forward to the bank, bent down and drank of the stream, and then offered up a heartfelt prayer of gratitude to God, who had thus far crowned his enterprise with signal success.

Sego, the chief town of the kingdom of Bambarra, Park found to consist of four separate and distinct divisions—two situated on the northern, and two on the southern bank of the river. The place contained as many as thirty thousand inhabitants, and, for a remote town in the heart of Africa, presented a wonderful aspect of substantiality and prosperity. Some of the houses were of two stories, and a number had their walls white-washed; the city streets were comparatively broad, and Moorish mosques rose in every direction. The river was thronged with canoes, the thoroughfares of the town crowded with foot-passengers, and the neighbouring country was so well cultivated as to excite considerable surprise in Mr. Park's mind.

Owing to the crowd of people desirous of being conveyed across the river, Mr. Park could not at once obtain a ferryman. While waiting his turn, seated on the bank of the river, he was informed that the king of Sego had refused to allow him to cross the river until he made known his object in visiting the country. A good deal discouraged by this rebuff, the traveller betook himself to a village at some distance from the town, where the king had bidden him take up his abode until further instructions.

THE NEGRO SONG. *Page 53.*

No one in the village would receive the traveller beneath his roof, and Mr. Park remained all day without food seated beneath a tree. The wind increased, there was every appearance of heavy rain, and the prospect of spending a night out-of-doors was a sufficiently dreary one, especially as the surrounding country was infested with wild animals.

At this juncture—when Park saw nothing before him but a night spent under these cheerless conditions—there occurred what was at once perhaps the most pleasing and not the least pathetic episode in all his African experiences. As it was growing dusk, a kind negro woman, returning from the fields, approached the faint and weary white man, and revealing in her looks her deep compassion for his sad plight, bade him follow her, while she herself carried his saddle and bridle. When she had seated Park on a mat in her hut, she trimmed a lamp, broiled a fish on the fire, and placed it before him as his supper. The rest of the household had meanwhile been watching the stranger with looks of wondering astonishment, but now resumed their occupation of spinning, which was continued far into the night. As they worked, the dark-skinned maidens sang to cheer their labour, and presently one improvised a song of which the white stranger was himself the theme. The air was sweet and plaintive, and the words touching in their naturalness and simplicity.

54   *PARK'S FIRST JOURNEY.*

* The words and music of the above song are taken from the original quarto edition of Park's travels. The words are by the Duchess of Devonshire, the music by G. G.

PARK'S FIRST JOURNEY.   55

I.

The loud wind roared, the rain fell fast,
The white man yielded to the blast;
He sat him down beneath our tree,
For weary, sad, and faint was he:
And ah, no wife, no mother's care,
For him the milk or corn prepare.

CHORUS.

The white man shall our pity share;
Alas! no wife or mother's care
For him the milk or corn prepare.

II.

The storm is o'er, the tempest past,
And Mercy's voice has hushed the blast;
The wind is heard in whispers low,
The white man far away must go;
But ever in his heart must bear
Remembrance of the negro's care.

CHORUS.

Go, white man, go—but with thee bear
The negro's wish, the negro's prayer,
Remembrance of the negro's care.

In perusing Mr. Park's journal no wonder is raised in the reader's mind, at this point, by the statement that the traveller was so keenly affected by the above episode that, weary though he was, sleep for long fled

Ferrari, a well-known composer of the day, who was thought to have succeeded admirably in retaining the simplicity and plaintiveness of the original melody, while giving it more body and shape.

from his eyes. To our thinking, there is an idyllic simplicity and even grace about the whole circumstances of the incident quite worthy to awaken the inspiration of the poet; while it is pleasing to contemplate in another and different light, as exemplifying how universal is the kindly bond of humanity that links the race together. Here surely was an instance of the " one touch of nature " that "makes the whole world kin."

The king of Sego's treatment of Park was, on the whole, liberal and considerate. He did not permit him to remain longer at Sego than two days; but in adopting this course he was greatly influenced, Mr. Park believed, by fear of the Moors. The traveller was, however, presented by the king with a bag containing five thousand cowries, and provided with a guide as far as Sansanding, his next halting-place. Sansanding was found to be a place of some importance, largely frequented by Moorish traders in beads and coral, gold-dust and cotton cloth. Here the traveller was first mistaken for some one else, and afterwards treated with much discourtesy and rudeness. The Moors gathered about him in great crowds, and insisted that he should accompany them to the mosque, and join in the Mohammedan worship. Mr. Park managed to escape this ordeal, but was compelled to mount a high seat in front of the mosque, in order that he might be easily seen by everybody.

Then the rabble crowded into the hut in which the traveller had taken up his lodging, for the purpose of watching him at his evening devotions and seeing him "eat eggs." Seven raw hen-eggs having been set before him, he had considerable difficulty in making it clear to the people that it was not the universal custom among Europeans to eat eggs uncooked—an idea which seemed rooted in their minds. To the wish of his visitors, that he should perform his devotions before them, he did not think fit to yield.

From his landlord at Sansanding, however, the traveller received hospitable enough treatment, which he in part repaid by writing out for the old man a *saphic* or charm, which the latter was very anxious to obtain. "If a Moor's saphic is good," said he, "a white man's must needs be better." Whereupon Mr. Park wrote out the charm of greatest virtue with which he was acquainted—the Lord's Prayer.

Quitting Sansanding, Park passed through Nyara and Nyamee, and presently his route again led through the forest. He was riding slowly on, his horse being greatly fatigued, when his guide suddenly exclaimed, "Wara billi billi" (A very large lion); and again, "Soubah an Allahi" (God preserve us). The traveller looked quickly round, and beheld a large red lion couching among the bushes a little way off from the track he was pursuing. Mr. Park feared every moment that the lion would spring upon him; but no such danger overtook him—the creature suffering him and his companion to pass quietly on.

At this stage of his journey the traveller suffered much from the attacks of mosquitoes, and passed night after night without obtaining sleep, engaged in a vain attempt to keep at bay the countless swarms of these remorseless insects. But a worse misfortune befell him in the necessity he was under of at length abandoning his horse, so long the faithful companion of his wanderings and the patient sharer of his every hardship. The poor animal had become too weak to proceed a yard further. All that Park could do was to place a bundle of grass before him and continue his journey on foot, heavy at heart for the loss of his horse, and with a dreary foreboding that a similar fate—death in the wilderness—awaited himself.

On reaching Kea, a small fishing village, Park embarked on the Niger in a canoe, and presently arrived at Moorzan, a town on the north bank of the river, whence he crossed over to Silla. Here, with much difficulty, he obtained lodging at the house of the dooty, and on the same night of his arrival in the town was prostrated with a sharp attack of fever.

Park's position was now a grave one. He was without clothing and without food, and possessed no means of procuring either. He was debilitated by frequent sickness, and by the long periods of fasting

A LION IN THE WAY.   Page 57.

which he had from time to time had to undergo. The difficulties of pushing his way further eastward were more than he could hope to overcome. The rainy season had already begun; in a little while the low grounds would be nothing else than marshes, and all progress, save by water, impossible. The few cowries still remaining to the traveller, from the king of Sego's present, were quite insufficient to hire a canoe for any length of time, and to trust to the good-will of the Moors for being forwarded on his way, Park knew, from painful experience, to be worse than vain. After long and anxious pondering of the question, he concluded that the only course left to him, if he was ever again to reach the coast a living man, was to turn his face westward; and no reader of his journal will for a moment doubt the wisdom of his decision, or dream of imputing a thought of faint-heartedness to the traveller for making it.

Park now began his return journey westward. At Modiboo an unexpected pleasure awaited him in the recovery of his horse, which had been found by the dooty of the place and restored to comparative strength. The traveller set out from Modiboo, driving his horse before him. The country was now little better than a swamp, and Mr. Park had to wade for miles together up to his knees in water. Twice his horse stuck fast in the mud, and was only disembedded with much difficulty. One morning the traveller counted fourteen native huts that had been undermined and wrecked since the rains had set in.

Mr. Park's reception at the several towns through which he now passed was the reverse of encouraging. The cause of this he was not long in discovering. A report had spread that he had come to Bambarra as a spy, and he was accordingly everywhere shunned and mistrusted. On his arrival at Sansanding, even Counti Mamadi, who, as he himself records, had received him so kindly on his eastward journey, now gave him but a cold welcome, and informed him that the king of Sego had sent after him to bring him back. Finally, Counti Mamadi advised Park to leave Sansanding early in the morning, and on no account to visit Diggani or any town near Sego.

Notwithstanding this caution, Park halted on August 11th at a small village within a short distance of the capital, where, however, the critical nature of his position being impressed upon him more strongly than ever, he resolved to avoid Sego altogether. Accordingly, mounting his horse, he struck into the swamps and forest again, and set his face due westward. More than once he had half resolved upon swimming the Niger, and making for Cape Coast to the south, but finally judged that he should carry out the object of his expedition more closely if he held on in a westerly direction, and sought to determine how far the Niger was navigable at that part of its course.

MEAT-MARKET AT YAMINA, ON THE NIGER.

Page 63.

Mr. Park's journey continued under difficulties. He suffered from scarcity of food, and from the toil and fatigue of travelling through the inundated country. On the 16th of August he passed through the town of Yamina. This he found to be a place of considerable importance; but as it was much frequented by the Moors, he did not think it safe to lodge in it.

On August the 18th he reached a narrow but rapid stream which he at first thought must be a tributary of the Niger, but presently discovered to be a distinct river. He entered the stream, leading his horse, and was already neck-deep in water, when a voice from the bank behind him loudly called upon him to come back. Turning round, Park beheld a native, who proceeded to inform him that the river was full of alligators, which would be certain to devour both the traveller and his horse if they tried to swim the river. When Mr. Park again stood on the bank, the black man, in great astonishment at this his first sight of a white man, exclaimed in a low voice, "God preserve us! who is this?" Mr. Park addressed the man in the Bambarra tongue, which seemed to reassure him; for he promised to help the traveller to cross the river. A canoe was procured, and in a short while Mr. Park was safely landed on the opposite bank.

The stranger's good offices did not cease here. At Taffara, Park, being unable to obtain a lodging, was seated beneath the bentang tree, exposed to the fierce violence of a storm that was then raging, when his former deliverer came up and shared his supper with the white man. He would have invited the traveller into the hut in which he was lodging; but being himself only a guest, he had not the authority. The night was spent by Park on the wet grass in an outer court.

Mr. Park had as much difficulty in procuring food for his horse as for himself. At the village of Sooha, the dooty absolutely refused to supply him with a morsel of either, whether for payment or charity. While the traveller was endeavouring to discover a reason for the man's unusually discourteous and rough bearing, the latter ordered a slave to bring a hoe. The slave began to dig a hole; the dooty meanwhile looking on, and muttering such sentences as, "Dank atoo" (Good for nothing), "Jankra lemen" (A real plague). When the slave had finished his work he departed to the village, and presently returned, carrying the dead body of a boy. In great surprise Park waited for the sequel. The slave, roughly lifting the naked corpse, flung it into the pit with a heartless indifference such as Mr. Park had never hitherto beheld during his travels. While the man threw in the earth over the grave, the dooty kept repeating, "Naphula attiniata" (Money lost), which left little doubt in Mr. Park's mind that the boy had been a slave. This was perhaps the most shocking scene witnessed by the traveller in Africa.

Pursuing his route along the bank of the river, he reached towards evening Koolikorro, a place of some size, the inhabitants of which traded extensively in salt. Here the native with whom he lodged, immediately on learning that the stranger was a Christian, proposed that Park should make him a saphic "to protect him from wicked men," promising that in return he would prepare for his guest a supper of rice. This was a chance of a good meal not to be lightly regarded by the half-famished wanderer. The landlord brought a board which Mr. Park covered with writing from top to bottom on both sides. What he wrote, on this occasion of charm-making, is not recorded in the traveller's journal; but whatever it was, it seemed abundantly to satisfy his landlord, who, washing off the writing on the board into a cup containing a little water, and murmuring a prayer over the liquid, drank it at a draught, afterwards licking the board dry, that no word of the potent charm might be wasted. That night our traveller enjoyed the only sufficient meal and good sleep he had had for many days.

On the 23rd of August Park reached Bammakoo, where he obtained from a slave-merchant information respecting his further route westward. What he learned was not reassuring. His road would lead him across the Joliba at a town where it would be impossible to procure a canoe large enough to convey his horse across the river. Mr. Park, however, had no alternative but to push forward. At Kooma, a secluded and picturesque village, he was most hospitably entertained by the simple and kind-hearted inhabitants, who brought a supper of corn and milk for the traveller, and provender for his horse, kindled his fire, and provided him with a hut for the night.

Mr. Park left Kooma escorted by two shepherds. Towards noon of the same day he heard a noise as of people shouting. Riding in the direction whence the sound proceeded he beheld a man seated on the stump of a tree, while some half-dozen heads were just visible among the grass. The traveller took the men for elephant-hunters, but they proved to be robbers—and of the most pitiless sort. Resistance would have been vain and probably dangerous. The traveller was stripped of everything he possessed, and at first feared that he would be left literally naked. But a spark of humanity survived even in the breasts of these savage banditti. They left their victim the oldest of his two shirts, a pair of trowsers, and his hat—for the recovery of which latter article Mr. Park was no doubt very thankful, as it was the receptacle of his notes.

This incident depressed Park more, probably, than any hardship he had yet endured. He was alone in a dreadful wilderness, almost naked, far away from all help from his own countrymen, with savage animals on every side, and men not less savage—a combination of adverse circumstances greater than he seemed able to struggle against. Thoughts of death filled his mind; there was nothing left for him but to lie down and breathe his last.

But in this his darkest hour, Park records that he was not entirely without support and solace. The thought that his present position was due to no fault or folly of his own, that he had fulfilled his mission to the best of his knowledge and ability, and that his fate was even now in the hands of that Providence who could protect him as surely in a strange land as in his own—these reflections came to sustain him, and prevented any feeling of bitterness mingling with his depression.

While he thus sat in sad contemplation of his fate, a trifling circumstance served to turn the current of his thoughts, to direct them into a more cheerful channel, and finally to fill his heart with fresh hope and courage. This happy reanimation of spirit was caused by the sight of a simple little plant, a small moss in fructification, the exquisite beauty of which had power to move the admiration of the traveller in his hour of deepest languor. Could the Being, he thought, who created this little plant, tended and nursed it to perfection in this remote spot, regard with indifference one of his own suffering children, made in his own likeness? Surely not! The thought forbade despair. The traveller rose from the ground, and battling down his hunger and fatigue, pressed onward in the hope that relief would yet reach him before it was too late. And he was not disappointed. Sufficient strength remained to him to enable him to reach Sibidooloo, the frontier town of Manding, at sunset.

In reading the above simple but affecting incident, it is impossible to avoid the thought of how a man's favourite study may sometimes come to his aid in the sorest strait. It is but one of many similar instances on record, as every reader of travel and biography must call to mind. To the love of all natural beauties with which Park's study of botany had inspired him the thoughts raised in his breast by the sight of the little flower must in part be attributed; for it is improbable that at such a moment a simple little moss-plant would have discovered all its delicate grace to an ordinary and untrained eye. This idea takes nothing from the moral side of the picture—the natural and devout emotions with which the sight of the flower filled the traveller's heart.

To the mansa—or chief man—of Sibidooloo, Park related his recent adventures, which roused in his hearer's breast an indignation creditable to him. "Sit down," said he; "you shall have everything restored to you.—Give the white man" (to an attendant) "a draught of water; and with the first light of the morning go over the hills, and inform the dooty of Bammakoo that a poor white man — the king of Bambarra's stranger — has been robbed by the king of Fooladoo's people."

Park remained two days at Sibidooloo, and no news of his horse and clothes having reached the town during that time, he resumed his journey. At Wonda he was obliged to rest as long as nine days, being stricken down with fever, from which he had suffered intermittently ever since the rainy season had set in. Food was now very scarce in every place through which the traveller passed, painful proofs of which he witnessed on all sides.

During his stay at Wonda, Park recovered his horse and clothes, sent on by the mansa of Sibidooloo, who had thus been enabled to redeem his promise. The traveller's compass, however, was so much broken as to be rendered useless; and his horse so emaciated that he was glad to be able to leave it with his landlord, who, he felt assured, would take every care of it.

Park was but partially recovered from his sickness when he resumed his march. Passing through several other villages and towns, he arrived at Kamalia, where he took up his residence at the house of one Karfa Taura, his acquaintance with whom proved of great importance to the traveller. Karfa Taura was a slave-merchant, and at the time of Park's arrival at Kamalia was collecting a *coffle* of slaves to take to the Gambia.

The traveller now saw an opportunity of obtaining an escort that was not to be lost. He found the slave-merchant, notwithstanding the nature of his calling, to be a man of an exceedingly reasonable and honest disposition. A compact was concluded, by the terms of which Karfa Taura was to allow Mr. Park to accompany him to the Gambia, supplying him with all necessary food on the journey; and in return for his services he was to receive the price of one slave.

Karfa Taura could not start on his journey until the rainy season was fairly over, and the roads in a condition for travelling by. Thus Mr. Park remained at Kamalia for a considerable time; and though during the greater part of his sojourn in the district he was prostrated with fever, he was able to collect a great deal of information in regard to the country and its inhabitants, all of which the reader will find detailed in the traveller's journal.

Nothing could exceed the kindness and attention bestowed upon Mr. Park, during this period, by Karfa Taura. He was provided with a comfortable hut, a mat-bed, an earthen jar for water, and a calabash cup; with everything, in fact, that is required in that simple and primitive society. Every day a slave brought him firewood and water, and two ample meals; and every day he was visited by his landlord in person, who came to inquire how it fared with the sick white man. Thus, when all but overcome by repeated disaster, hunger, and illness, Mr. Park was succoured and delivered by this benevolent negro.

At length, on April 19th, Karfa Taura was ready to set out with his coffle of slaves—thirty-five in number. It will easily be understood how the remainder of Mr. Park's journey was beset with far fewer perils, hardships, and vicissitudes than the first portion of it had been. He was now accompanied by a strong escort; food was forthcoming regularly and in sufficient quantity; and the roads no longer presented the same almost insurmountable obstacles to progress which they had formerly done. The Jallonka wilderness was that part of the route which proved the most fatiguing and the most dangerous; fatiguing from its vastness and the density of the forest, and dangerous from the number of wild beasts infesting it.

The route pursued by the caravan led across the Bafing or Black River, one of the principal branches of the Senegal. This stream was crossed on a very curiously constructed bridge of bamboo—a sort of floating bridge formed by two high trees, which, when fastened together by their topmost boughs, stretched from one bank of the river to the other. When a few trees are placed in this position and laid with bamboos, the whole forms a gangway sloping down from each end towards the middle. Such a bridge is well adapted to a stream liable to be flooded every season, since it can be so quickly and easily constructed.

After passing through many towns and villages the caravan at length reached the Gambia, and on the 10th of June 1797 Mr. Park was once more in Pisania, where, it needs not to be said, he was welcomed with the greatest joy—not the less keen because he had been almost given up for dead. Dr. Laidley discharged the traveller's debt to Karfa Taura with large interest, giving the negro twice the sum agreed upon. Though Karfa Taura had amply deserved this liberal treatment, his kindness towards Mr. Park having continued to the last, he was greatly overcome by the additional recompense. The whole European life at Pisania, moreover, made a manifest impression on him; and more than once he exclaimed to Mr. Park, with a thoughtful look and a sigh: "Fato fing inta feng" (Black men are nothing).

Mr. Park reached England by a somewhat indirect route, embarking in an American ship, the *Charlestown*, on the 15th of June. He was delayed for ten days on the island of Antigua, and did not arrive in England until the end of November.

The pleasure of Mr. Park's friends, and, it may be said, of the people of England generally, at his safe return, hardly exceeded their astonishment; for all hopes of the traveller being still alive were beginning to be abandoned. Two years had passed without any word of him having reached England. As may be imagined, the interest excited by the story he had to

BAMBOO BRIDGE ACROSS THE BAFING.
Page 73.

tell was very great among almost all classes of the community. The African Association were as proud as they were pleased at the success of the expedition which had been originated and equipped under their auspices; and the general public were eager to hear the stirring tale of travel, adventure, and discovery.

Park's journey, both in its character and results, was the most important that had yet been accomplished. The traveller had beheld the Niger, and had definitely determined, past all doubt and question, the direction of the great river for a large portion of its course. He had also collected a mass of information regarding Central Africa, which, though not absolutely trustworthy, as subsequent discovery has proved, as far exceeded in accuracy as it did in amount the work of any previous discoverer.

CHAPTER III.

PARK'S SECOND JOURNEY.

SOON after arriving in England, Park set about the task of arranging and writing the journal of his travels—a work which cost him much time and pains.

The conditions of his journey, it may be imagined, were not favourable to literary composition, and the notes made on the way were, accordingly, meagre and disjointed; so that Park had to rely greatly on his memory, which was fortunately a retentive one. The labour of authorship, moreover, was one which he had never before essayed, and composition came only with pains. But he was rewarded for the conscientious care which he bestowed upon his book by its large sale when published; for it rapidly won its way in the popular favour, and brought its author both fame and profit.

Park now settled down into private life, establishing himself as a doctor in Peebles. There he performed faithfully and diligently the usual duties of a country surgeon, doing much hard work for sufficiently scanty pay. It is worth noting that during this period he made the acquaintance of Sir Walter Scott, the two men becoming excellent friends. The novelist greatly admired the character of the traveller, and has recorded his opinion of it in warm terms in the "Surgeon's Daughter."

But though Park conscientiously fulfilled his professional duties in Peebles, there were many indications that his heart really lay in other work. His thoughts continually went out to the great river of which he could justly regard himself as the discoverer, but which still lay hid in so much vagueness and mystery. He longed to complete the work he had begun—to possess the whole secret of the Niger. He was constantly revolving in his mind the project of a second African expedition, which should crown his previous labours, and set at rest every geographical problem connected with Central Africa.

It was some time ere Park's hopes and ambitions seemed likely to be gratified; but at length the chance he had been waiting for arrived. The English Government determined upon sending an expedition to Central Africa, and Park was asked to lead it. After some delay, caused mainly by a change in the administration of the country, Mr. Park was ready to set out. He sailed from Portsmouth on the 30th of January 1805, having as companions Mr. Anderson, his brother-in-law; and Mr. Scott, the draughtsman of the expedition. At Goree he secured the services of an officer and thirty-five soldiers, who, with some half-dozen artificers and two qualified seamen, completed the party.

At Kayee, Park engaged as guide to the expedition Isaaco, a Mandingo merchant and priest—a man well qualified for the office by his knowledge of inland travelling. Pisania was reached on April 28th; and here Mr. Park and his comrades were warmly received by Mr. Ainsley, who had been of so much assistance to the traveller on his former journey.

The expedition set out from Pisania on the 4th of May. Mr. Park divided his men into six messes. Mr. Scott marched with the first division, under whose guidance were the asses; Lieutenant Martyn had charge of the centre; while Mr. Park himself, together with Mr. Anderson, brought up the rear. Thus the party proceeded, marching by day and pitching their tents at night. May the 11th brought them to Medina, the chief town of Woolli, where Park had to pay a heavy tax of amber and coral to the king.

At Tambico, Isaaco the guide was plundered, maltreated, and made a prisoner, being at length released only by a ransom of considerable value. Shortly after this the party suffered a strange but serious enough attack from a large swarm of bees, whose onslaught was of such violence that six of the asses and one horse died from the effects of their stings.

The tribute which the various native kings enforced from Mr. Park was greater than he had anticipated; indeed it may be said that the mission was literally plundered on every hand. Difficulties of other kinds, too, soon began to beset it, and to increase with every stage of its progress. The rains set in, and the health of the men began rapidly to deteriorate. This eventuality Park had clearly foreseen; but on various accounts he had not deemed it advisable to delay his journey until after the wet season.

In the beginning of June the first death occurred—that of a carpenter. A few days later a succession of tornadoes, each of exceeding violence, was experienced, exercising an immediate and marked effect for the worse upon the health of the soldiers. This, to use Park's own brief fateful words, was *the beginning of sorrows*.

Fever and dysentery were soon making havoc among the men. No one wholly escaped—the leader himself suffering with the rest—and before the month was over a sad gap was visible in the little party. During this period of dire distress, the best qualities of the leader shone out conspicuously. Patient, self-denying, undaunted, often enduring fatigue that his comrades might be spared it, and foregoing rest that they might have the more, cheering the sick and soothing the dying, Park won the affection and admiration of all.

On the 4th of July, Isaaco narrowly escaped being devoured by a crocodile. As he was crossing with some of the asses the river Wonda, a tributary of the Senegal, an alligator caught him by the leg and dragged him under. The black man instantly drove his finger into the creature's eye; the brute's grip relaxed, and the guide made for the shore. But he was not quick enough for his enemy, which once more seized him. Isaaco turned, and this time thrust his fingers into both eyes of the crocodile, which at once quitted its hold and presently swam down the stream. But Isaaco's wounds were of so serious a character that the party were obliged to halt for four days before he was able to proceed.

On the 19th, the Ba Woolima, a tributary of the Senegal, was reached, and safely crossed, after much difficulty, by means of an extemporized bridge cleverly constructed by the negroes out of two large trees and a number of forked sticks.

Almost daily the expedition dwindled away before the extreme hardships and difficulties of the journey—chief among which were the fatal effects of the climate. By the 19th of August only one-fourth of the party survived. Some, at their own request, had been left on the road to die, among whom was Mr. Scott. Mr. Anderson was soon to follow; but he had the sad satisfaction of at least beholding the Niger from afar. At Leniba, from the summit of a range of hills which stretches between the Niger and the Senegal, the surviving members of the expedition saw the great river "rolling its immense stream along the plain."

The sight of the river, which was the goal of their journey, inspired the little band with fresh strength and courage, and they ventured to hope that their hardships were almost at an end. Several more men died, however, before Bammakoo was reached, where the party embarked in a canoe on the Niger. On the following day they arrived at Marraboo, where Isaaco's engagement with the expedition ceased. He was paid the reward agreed upon for his services; and a second compact was then made between him and Mr. Park, to the effect that he was to receive all the asses and horses if he should succeed in securing for the expedition the protection of the king of Bambarra and permission to build a boat.

Isaaco set out on his mission, and some days passed before any word came from Bambarra. Park was harassed with doubt and perplexity, but was presently relieved by the arrival of an envoy from Sego, the capital of Bambarra, who announced that the king would be glad to receive the expedition, and accept from Mr. Park whatever remaining presents he proposed to make.

The reception which the expedition received at Sego was on the whole reassuring. The king promised to sell Mr. Park a canoe; and after great difficulty and delay a suitable vessel was got ready. Mr. Anderson was never to embark in the *Joliba*—the name which was given to the canoe. On the 28th he breathed his last. Park's grief and dejection at the death of his brother-in-law exceeded in intensity all other misfortunes that had befallen him during his journey. "No event," he writes, "that took place during the journey ever threw the smallest gloom over my mind, till I laid Mr. Anderson in the grave. I then felt myself a second time lonely and friendless amidst the wilds of Africa."

The party now included five white men only. Though now fairly embarked on the Niger, Park, after coming through an experience of so much disaster and distress, could not but be filled with the most anxious forebodings. Still no sign of flinching from his purpose escaped him. His courage and calmness remained unshaken. "Though all the Europeans who are with me should die, and though I were myself half dead, I would still persevere." Thus he writes to Lord Camden; while his letters to his wife express a like resolution to persevere to the death, together with a confident hope in the ultimate success of his enterprise.

Park began his last voyage down the Niger on November 17th, 1805. It was long ere any further intelligence of the traveller and his comrades reached

England. At last Park's friends became anxious about him, and the governor of Sierra Leone, Colonel Maxwell, despatched Isaaco the guide to inquire after the fate of the expedition. At Sansanding, Isaaco met Amadi Fatouma, the man who had taken his place as guide and enterpreter to the expedition, and received from his hands papers which described the voyage of the Englishmen down the river.

Park and his companions reached Silla and Jenne in safety; but at Kabra, the port of Timbuctoo, and at Gousamo, they were attacked by the natives, who were only repelled by a sharp musket-fire. At Sawer, Amadi Fatouma quitted the party, his engagement ceasing at that town. Immediately thereafter he was seized and imprisoned by the king, on the pretext that the expedition had entered his dominions without making him sufficient presents. Next morning a large battalion of troops was sent forward to intercept the English party.

The native soldiers took up their position at Boussa, at a point where the river flowed through a narrow and rocky pass. When the English party attempted to sail this narrow channel, they were attacked by the native troops with spears, arrows, and stones. The little band of Englishmen defended themselves vigorously for some time; but at length, believing that all chance of getting through the channel was over, Park caught hold of one of his comrades and leaped with him into the river. Lieutenant Martyn followed the example of his leader, and all were drowned while attempting to escape by swimming. The natives who escaped from the canoe narrated the circumstances of the final catastrophe to Amadi Fatouma upon the release of the latter from his imprisonment three months later.

Isaaco was absent on his mission for fully twenty months, and such was the story he brought back with him to Sierra Leone. Nearly a quarter of a century later Captain Clapperton, and after him Richard and John Lander, obtained such evidence in regard to the manner of Park's death as placed the truth of Amadi Fatouma's statement almost beyond a doubt.

Thus terminated an expedition conceived under hopeful and even brilliant auspices, but opposed by disaster from the very beginning; and thus its gallant and noble leader perished.

The witness of friends is unanimous as to the character of Mungo Park; but such testimony is not needed. The man is manifest in his life, and a perusal of his journal reveals to any but the most undiscerning reader what manner of person the great traveller was. He possessed every qualification for the arduous task which he undertook and so successfully accomplished; for his intrepid courage was mingled with the quiet strength of patience, his ardour united with a calm prudence, his enthusiasm balanced

FACSIMILE OF
SKETCH MAP
OF
MUNGO PARK'S
INTENDED ROUTE
IN HIS SECOND EXPEDITION
TO THE NIGER.

From a Drawing by himself.

Senegal River

Bambara

Jeenie or Genne

Mafina
Canfanding
Yamina
serinum ---- Sego

Joliba River or Niger

by a shrewd, practical common sense. He was as completely fitted morally as he was mentally and physically for the great work of his life; and we make bold to say, without fear of challenge, that in no traveller before or since will there be found a happier union and a finer equipoise of the qualities essential to a hero of discovery.

From our narrative the reader may gather how Park bore himself in the chief crises of his two arduous and perilous journeys; but he must seek the journal itself for a full and clear revelation of the traveller's character. We have referred to the fact that the work of composition came with difficulty to him, but nevertheless the journal is a model of what such a work should be. It is written in an easy and natural yet animated style, in correct and idiomatic English, and with a judgment and good taste that are conspicuous. There is not a vain or boastful line, not a self-pitying or impatient sentence in all the book; and this in a record of so much vicissitude, hardship, and peril met and overcome. You learn the traveller's undaunted courage only from his acts—as simply narrated as they are possible to be; and the modesty of the writer is everywhere as noticeable as his courage. No one of the innumerable narratives of travel and adventure that have appeared since leave a more pleasing impression on the reader than the journal of Mungo Park.

CHAPTER IV.

CLAPPERTON AND THE LANDERS.

In our epitome of African discovery thus far we have followed the plan adopted by Mr. Hugh Murray*—that, namely, of giving an unbroken and consecutive narrative of Park's travels; the reader being thus enabled to survey the traveller's career in an uninterrupted sequence. Between Park's first and second expedition, however, several journeys of exploration were made into Central Africa by various travellers. The most important of these was that undertaken by Frederick Horneman, a young German student, who set out from Egypt in the company of a caravan in 1798. Mr. Horneman was equipped for his expedition by the African Association. At Siwah, an oasis on the way to Fezzan, the traveller came upon some very singular and ancient ruins, a portion of which some have conjectured to be the remains of the famous temple of Jupiter Ammon. Later in his journey he was threat-

---

* No one who attempts to treat the subject of African discovery can fail to be under obligations to Mr. Hugh Murray, to whose labours and skill we here acknowledge with gratitude our own indebtedness.

ened with death at the hands of the Arabs, but his remarkable coolness and presence of mind saved him. He was so well versed not only in the Mohammedan language, but in the tenets of the faith, that, with a little adroitness and assurance, he succeeded in making the natives believe that he too was a Moslem.

After a difficult and fatiguing journey of sixteen days, Horneman arrived at Fezzan, where he proposed to collect information regarding the Niger and Timbuctoo. He subsequently visited Tripoli, and then a period of two years passed without any further word of the traveller reaching England. He was next heard of as being at Kashna; and Major Denham, during his expedition, ascertained that he had died at Nyffe on the Niger, stricken down by the climate.

Horneman was succeeded in the work of African exploration by Mr. Nicholls, who died of fever on the threshold of his journey. Roentgen, a German, followed, to encounter a fate equally brief and sad. His body was found a little way from his starting-point, and the probability is that he was murdered by his guides. Thus three lives, in quick succession, were added to the roll of victims to the cause of African discovery.

The narrative now falls to be resumed at the period after Park's second journey. Fatal in its issue as that expedition had been, there were many circumstances connected with it calculated rather to stimulate than depress the public interest in African exploration. Several problems in regard to Central Africa still awaited solution;—the exact course of the Niger throughout its whole extent, and the relation of the same river to the Congo; were the two rivers in part identical, or wholly distinct?

To endeavour to determine these points, a twin expedition was despatched to Africa under Government auspices in 1816. It was under the command of Major Peddie and Captain Tuckey. Major Peddie was to descend the Niger, Captain Tuckey to ascend the Congo. The expedition encountered difficulties and disaster almost from the outset, and had at last to be abandoned. A similar fate befell Captain Grey, who in 1818 made a gallant but unsuccessful attempt to follow Park's route.

Nothing further of importance was accomplished until the missions of Major Denham and Lieutenant Clapperton in 1821, which proposed to explore Central Africa, with Tripoli as a starting-point. The expedition divided itself into two parties—the plan that had been resolved on being that each should pursue a separate route and meet again at an agreed point. Major Denham's journey proved a most varied and adventurous one, and furnished a great deal of fresh and interesting information regarding the country traversed. But Denham's discoveries did not bear directly upon the Niger, and must, therefore, in the comparatively limited space at our disposal, be excluded from our narrative. The two journeys made by Lieutenant Clapperton, however, fall to be treated in more detail.

When Clapperton parted from his *confrère*, Major Denham, he travelled westward in company with Dr. Oudney, the second in command of the party. At Murmur Dr. Oudney died, and Clapperton pushed on alone. After five weeks of travel Kano was reached —a large and important town of thirty thousand inhabitants, carrying on an extensive and varied commerce with all parts of Africa. Clapperton found the markets of Kano filled with a profusion of articles whose richness and variety astonished him,—cloth of every description, raw silk, linen from Egypt embroidered with gold, Moorish dresses, Maltese swordblades, tin and antimony, ornaments in glass, coral, silver, and pewter, besides live stock and farm and garden produce, and everywhere long rows of slaves.

Lieutenant Clapperton next halted at Sackatoo, a large and substantially built town. Here he made handsome presents to Sultan Bello—a chief described as being of stately appearance, with a grand head and fine dark eyes. He received the expedition well, and showed himself to be possessed of an inquiring mind, and a degree of enlightenment much beyond his order.

On the advice of this chief, Clapperton resolved to

proceed no further at present than Sackatoo, having become convinced that the route to the Gulf of Benin was impracticable. Before finally leaving Sackatoo he gathered such information in regard to Park's death as convinced him that Amadi Fatouma's story was in all essential particulars true. At Kouka he rejoined Major Denham; and the two travellers, having each accomplished a long and arduous journey, fruitful in interesting discoveries, reached England in June 1825, after an absence of nearly four years.

The results of Denham and Clapperton's expeditions were sufficiently encouraging to induce the British Government to equip another mission in the very year of the travellers' return. Clapperton—now a Captain—was chosen as leader, with Captain Pearce and Mr. Morrison as his colleagues in command. The party started on their journey from Badagry early in December. The start was most disastrous; for the travellers having slept a night in the open air were presently prostrated with fever and ague. Mr. Morrison was obliged to give up the idea of accompanying the expedition, and died on the way back to the ship. Captain Pearce struggled on bravely a little longer, but at last succumbed; and Captain Clapperton, himself much weakened by his sickness, pursued his journey under peculiarly lonely and depressing conditions. But he had one faithful and devoted companion left in his servant Richard Lander, whose name in connection with African discovery was one day to become even more famous than that of his master.

A march of sixty miles brought the little party to Yarriba, where the travellers were most favourably received, the people flocking to meet them in every town through which they passed, and signifying the honour in which they held the white men by dancing, festivals, and merry-making.

The next place of importance reached was Tshow. Here the expedition was overtaken by a bodyguard sent on by the king of Yarriba, consisting of a number of the royal troops dressed in the most fantastic of uniforms, and presenting a wild and formidable appearance beyond description.

At Katunga, Captain Clapperton had an audience of the king of Yarriba, who received the Englishmen seated in a veranda. The monarch wore a pasteboard crown, two long *tobes*, or mantles, of cotton cloth, and a profusion of glass-bead ornaments. He was surrounded by troops of his wives—more in number than Captain Clapperton could account—who welcomed the stranger with great cheering, smiling on him the while with the utmost graciousness.

Captain Clapperton found Yarriba to be a flourishing and prosperous kingdom, justly and leniently governed, and practising few of the dark and barbarous customs common in Ashantee and Dahomey and many neighbouring states. Polygamy, to be sure, largely prevails. And when Captain Clapperton assured several of the chief men of Katunga that the king of England had but one wife, the statement was received with mingled amazement and pity that so great a sovereign should be in so forlorn and desolate a case. The king of Yarriba was proud to think that his own wives, hand joined in hand, would stretch from one end of his dominions to the other.

From Yarriba Clapperton passed into the Borgoo country, presently arriving at the city of Kiama, an important place of thirty thousand inhabitants. The party was met by the king himself, accompanied by a peculiar but striking bodyguard. Six young girls wearing girdles of beads, and with their hair bound with fillets, ran beside the king's horse, each maiden brandishing three spears. As they ran they bounded and leaped with a lightness and agility that had the appearance of flying, while their motions were as full of grace as swiftness, and their eyes sparkled with vivacity. By-and-by the damsels, laying aside their lances, robed themselves in blue mantles and waited on the king.

After departing from Kiama, Captain Clapperton and his companions reached Wa-wa. Here the most amusing episode certainly in the whole journey occurred. A certain wealthy widow, called Zuma, conceived a violent affection for the leader of the expedition, whom she favoured with a degree of attention that became nothing short of persecution. The widow, though little past her twentieth year, was a lady of more than *embonpoint*—of such ample proportions, in fact, that Captain Clapperton could find no fitter comparison for her than a " walking tun-butt." This pronounced style of beauty Zuma emphasized by her manner of dressing, loading her person with bright and gaudy finery, and a profusion of ornaments of gold, coral, and beads; while her hair she dyed blue, her eyebrows black, and her hands and feet red.

Thus equipped, the widow laid siege to Captain Clapperton's heart, which, however, remained proof against her most cunning blandishments. Finding the chief of the expedition impregnable, she directed the battery of her smiles upon his lieutenant and servant Richard Lander; but with a like result. Lander was an extremely prudent and cool-tempered young man; and Zuma's charms, which were still noticeable notwithstanding her extreme plumpness, made no impression upon him. The lady now renewed her attack upon Captain Clapperton with fresh energy, and nothing short of flight from Wa-wa rid the Englishman of her persecutions. Signs were not wanting that other considerations besides those of affection influenced the widow's action. It was rumoured that she cherished ambitious designs of supplanting the king upon his throne—a project in which she trusted to be materially aided by marriage with a young and brave Englishman. Altogether, Captain Clapperton experienced a very decided feeling of relief when he was finally rid of this ambitious and redoubtable African beauty.

Clapperton presently visited Boussa, the scene of Park's death; but sufficient reference has already been made to this episode in his journey. Crossing the Niger, and passing through Nyffe, the mission arrived at Zeg-zeg, an exceedingly fertile region, beautifully wooded, and rich with meadow and corn-land.

The next halt was at Kano, Clapperton's old quarters, which he now found in all the distress and confusion of war. The king of Bornou was at deadly feud with the Fellata, and the travellers beheld signs of battle on every side. At the sultan's advice Captain Clapperton betook himself with his companions to Sackatoo, and was there lodged in the same hut which he had formerly occupied. This was the traveller's last halting-place. It was not to be permitted him to complete the journey which he had thus far carried through with such intrepidity and with so much success. He was exhausted by illness; but other causes besides bodily weakness combined to depress him.

The kindly and sympathetic attitude of the natives towards the English mission, which we saw so conspicuously displayed during Captain Clapperton's previous journey, had now changed to a feeling of suspicion and distrust. A rumour, entirely without foundation, was abroad throughout Houssa that the British nation meditated an invasion of the country. Influenced by this idea, King Bello now acted with great discourtesy and harshness towards Captain Clapperton, seizing by force a letter which he was bearing to the king of Bornou. Clapperton bitterly resented this treatment, and spoke his mind out very freely to the king; which only had the effect of still further irritating the jealous and angry prince. The Englishman was detained as a prisoner, and even threatened with personal violence; but matters did not reach this extreme.

Thus disappointment and vexation, chafing Clapperton's eager and brave spirit, united with sickness to wear out a frame already debilitated by the long effects of an African climate. He was prostrated with dysentery, which presently took a fatal development. The closing scenes of the traveller's life form a very touching picture. He was nursed day and night by his servant Richard Lander with more than a woman's watchfulness and gentle care. Towards the end the dying man called Lander to his side.

"Richard, I shall shortly be no more. I feel myself dying," he said.

Almost choked with grief, Lander could only reply, "God forbid, my dear master; you will live many years yet."

"Don't be so much affected, my dear boy, I entreat you," answered Clapperton. "It is the will of the Almighty; it cannot be helped."

Then the dying master proceeded to instruct his attendant in regard to his journals and the course he wished him to pursue after he was dead. Finally, taking Lander's hand in his own, he gazed into his face, and with his eyes moist with tears said in low and deeply-affected voice,—

"My dear Richard, if you had not been with me I should have died long ago. I can only thank you with my latest breath for your kindness and attachment to me; and if I could have lived to return with you, you should have been placed beyond the reach of want; but God will reward you."

A few days later the brave traveller quietly breathed his last. The strong attachment which existed between Clapperton and Lander is evident in various letters from the former to the latter, in which the master expresses an affectionate desire for the welfare and happiness of his servant most pleasing to contemplate. Clapperton was a kind and large-hearted man, as well as one of most fearless courage, capable of great patience under difficulty and disaster, and of a bright and buoyant temperament that carried him lightly through many a delicate and trying situation.

After Clapperton's death King Bello's attitude towards the expedition softened somewhat. He allowed Lander to bury his master quietly and decently, suffered him to depart from the country, and even forwarded him on his homeward route. After a journey of considerable vicissitude and danger, in the course of which he made a praiseworthy but unsuccessful attempt to discover the termination of the Niger, Richard Lander reached the coast, and arrived in England in April 1828.

Brief mention must in this place be made of Major Laing's journey to Timbuctoo, which was contemporaneous with Clapperton's second expedition. During his short stay at Timbuctoo, Laing was able to add materially to our knowledge of the topography of the district. The traveller's journey had the same tragic and sad ending as that of so many of his predecessors. He was murdered by his guide, a Moorish merchant, who had undertaken to conduct him to the coast.

It will be seen that there still existed much uncertainty in regard to the course of the Niger. What was accurately known was this:—In his first journey, Park had traced the course of the river between Bammakoo and Silla, and had also ascertained that it rose in the same mountainous range as the Senegal. In his second expedition he determined the river's course below Silla as far as Timbuctoo. Clapperton had fixed the position of Boussa *beyond Timbuctoo*, but the actual course of the river *between those two towns* remained still to be explored. It was reserved for Richard and John Lander to determine this still undiscovered portion of the great river. The three most famous names connected with the Niger are undoubtedly those of Park, and Richard and John Lander, if we regard the work accomplished from the point of view of its success. The Landers, in a word, completed what Park had begun; and the important results of their expedition, as well as its intrinsic interest, deserve that it should be treated with as much detail as our remaining space will allow.

The British Government having resolved to equip an expedition for the purpose of exploring the Niger below Boussa, Richard Lander volunteered his services as its leader. He was accompanied by his younger brother John, to whom a due measure of the honour of the expedition must in justice be accorded, and who not only shared with his elder brother every toil and hardship, but materially assisted him with his journals.

The brothers sailed from England in January 1830, and arrived at Cape Coast Castle towards the end of the following month. Accompanied by a small party of natives and the interpreter Pascoe, they reached Badagry on the 21st of March. Here they remained for several days, detained by the king, whose rapacity would not permit him to let the Englishmen quit his dominions while he could extract from them another present.

This region the travellers describe as a fertile and beautiful one, but its people as idle, covetous, and lax in moral tone. Their religion is largely the Mohammedan; and the Landers, during their sojourn in Badagry, witnessed certain of their ceremonial observances.

The *ensemble* of the scene presented a spectacle of no little interest, from its novelty and strangeness. On a sandy tract of ground encircled by trees the travellers discovered a number of Mussulmans in the act of ablution and worship. Every company of fresh arrivals was greeted by a burst of music from a native band. Every one wore his gayest bravery—loose mantles, caps and turbans in the greatest variety, and of the gaudiest colours; while the scarfs and aprons of the worshippers glittered with golden embroidery and silver spangles. At the conclusion of the ceremony, drums, bells, and fifes combined with volleys of musketry to raise a deafening din.

The chief industry of Badagry is fishing, together with yam and maize growing. The fish is taken either with the net or by spearing, or by a curious and ingenious earthenware pot baited with palm oil. The huts of the natives are of neat construction, made of bamboo, and roofed with palm leaves.

The travellers left Badagry on the last day of March in a canoe lent them by the king, Adooley. Slowly they glided in their long narrow vessel down the silent river, a starry sky and a bright moon guiding them on their way. The scenery was wild and picturesque, but could not be described as grand, the river banks being low and partially wooded with small trees, varied ever and anon by one of larger growth—a majestic palm rising in solitary grandeur, its stately plume of foliage waving softly in the night wind. Now and then a slave-factory or a fetich-hut was noted as the canoe floated noiselessly on.

In a little while the river narrowed to a breadth of not more than twenty yards, while its surface became covered with a wealth of marine plants, from which there arose, in a dense cloud, a reeking and noxious miasma. But the stream again broadened, the floating plants disappeared, the vegetation on the banks grew richer and more beautiful, until the trees were so thick that they formed an arch above the heads of the voyagers that effectually shielded them from the hot sun. The river now abounded with alligators and hippopotami, while monkeys and parrots, wild ducks and other birds, were seen on all sides.

On the 6th of April the two brothers reached Jenne, where they were hospitably entertained by the governor. The inhabitants of this district are described as temperate and diligent—diligent, that is, for a people dwelling in a land where but a slight amount of labour yields a sufficient sustenance for daily wants.

Katunga was reached on the 13th of May. King

RIVER SCENE IN WESTERN AFRICA.

Page 106.

Mansolah received the mission favourably. On the occasion of the travellers' first audience with this chief he was dressed in a style of great, though somewhat incongruous, magnificence. His crown resembled in shape a bishop's mitre, and was decorated with a profusion of coral beads, and secured beneath the chin to prevent it from falling off. His mantle was a wonderful patchwork of green silk, crimson damask, and green velvet. His feet were clad in English cotton stockings, and native sandals of neat workmanship; and beneath him was spread a carpet of fine blue cloth, the gift of Captain Clapperton.

In the end of May the expedition halted at Kiama, entering a region whose people differed in many respects — in language, customs, and religion — from those among whom their route had hitherto led them. Here the brothers were accommodated in a large circular hut, the centre support of which was composed of the stem of a tree. Two apertures gave entrance and egress to the hut, over which charms were suspended as a security against fire, much in the same way as horse-shoes are still, in our enlightened England, nailed up over barn doors for "luck." The walls of the cabin were covered with bows and quivers, guns, swords, spears, and other weapons. Outside, the scene was sufficiently novel and striking. Although a thunderstorm was at its height, native men, women, and children were seated in groups on the ground, or gathered about several large fires asleep. The men carried their weapons by their sides, and their horses grazed near at hand, while the lurid firelight lit up the half-naked figures of all.

Presently entering Kiama, the Landers had an audience of King Yarro, who received them alone, seated on buffalo hides. The walls of the room were decorated with well-executed prints of King George the Fourth, the Duke of York, Lord Nelson, the Duke of Wellington, and a portrait of a gaily-dressed and smiling English lady. Here and there on the walls were fastened ragged scraps of paper inscribed with passages from the Koran. The floor was strewn confusedly with muskets, handsomely ornamented spears, and other weapons of war.

The travellers, departing from Kiama, reached a place called Kakafungi, a large straggling town, finely situated on a level plain, the inhabitants of which were so clean in their persons, so well-mannered, and possessed of such neat and comfortable houses, that the Englishmen were immediately prepossessed in their favour. These first impressions were but strengthened by the subsequent conduct of the Kakafungians. The travellers were provided with a capital hut, and their entertainers waited on them in a body, bringing with them two kids and an ample supply of corn and milk, the whole being presented by a little band of boys and girls!

On the 17th of June, Boussa was reached—an important stage in the journey, by reason of the interesting relics of Mr. Park which were here discovered. As the two brothers sat on the rocky promontory overlooking the spot where Park and his comrades met their death, serious and sad thoughts could not but arise in their breasts, as they recalled the fate not only of the peerless explorer Park himself, but of the many gallant men who had followed in his track and sacrificed their lives for the same end—the endeavour to unriddle the mystery of the strange and fateful river on whose waters they were now gazing.

The travellers received from a native a tobe of rich crimson damask, stiff with the quantity of gold embroidery upon it, which there was strong evidence to prove had belonged to Mr. Park. A day or two later the travellers received a visit from the king, bringing with him a book said to have been recovered from the water after the upsetting of the canoe which held Park and his companions. The volume was wrapped up in a cotton cloth, and was of considerable size. The hopes of the Landers rose high that the book would prove to be Mr. Park's journal, and their disappointment was proportionately great on discovering that it was only an obsolete nautical treatise. Between the leaves, however, a few slight relics of the great traveller were found—one or two papers of no intrinsic importance, but bearing his handwriting and signature.

Some days afterwards, at Yaoorie, a gun which had been Mr. Park's was also recovered, one of the Landers giving his own in exchange for it to an Arab in whose possession it was.

After some delay two canoes were procured by the brothers, for their return voyage from Yaoorie. Boussa was again reached on the 5th of August; and the Landers now resolved to make for Wowou, to procure a vessel better adapted for their purpose than those which they at present possessed. They were ultimately successful in this plan, though the arrival of the canoe promised them by the king of Wowou did not take place until the middle of the following month. On the 20th of September, everything being at length in readiness, the explorers embarked from Boussa in two canoes. But a short span of their voyage was accomplished when it was discovered that the smaller of the canoes was extremely leaky and in risk of sinking; and at midday therefore a halt had to be made at a little island called Melalie, in order to cobble up the boat. The next camping-place was on a large and beautiful island called Patashie, remarkably rich and fertile, and shady with groves of magnificent palms.

Having procured a water-tight canoe, the voyagers were once more afloat upon the river, and for some distance sailed on without delay or hindrance. Arriving at Lever, or, as the town is frequently called, Layaba, they remained till the beginning of October.

Here the channel of the Niger was deep and clear, and its breadth from one to three miles.

On October the 4th a large town was reached called Bajiebo, to which the Landers give the palm among African towns for confusion and dirt, and disagreeables of every description. Here the travellers saw canoes of a peculiar description, different from any they had yet met with. They were large, made each of a single tree-stem, and bulwarked high with planks. Many of the canoes had huts built on them, thatched with straw, in which whole families lived together, carrying on their whole household operations.

On October 6th, on departing from the island of Madjie, where the travellers had camped for the night, they journeyed swiftly down the river, and presently came suddenly in sight of a lofty and picturesque rock called Mount Kesa; which, rising sheer from the water to a height of three hundred feet, cone-shaped and girdled with stately trees, made an exceedingly noble and imposing feature in the landscape.

The voyagers next reached the island of Belee, where they had an interview with the chief, an important personage in his own estimation, and rejoicing in a high-sounding but not unpoetical title—the *King of the Dark Water*. This chieftain made an imposing approach to the travellers. A sound of men singing was heard in the distance, then the dip of paddles keeping time to the voices, but still nothing was seen.

Presently a canoe came in sight, then a second and much larger one, rowed by a score of stalwart youths, who sang as they rowed. The travellers were surprised at the "pomp and circumstance" of the whole procession, the royal barge being gaily ornamented with awnings and scarlet cloth embroidered with gold lace. Three or four young pages, becomingly attired, stood at the prow, and in the stern a band of handsome musicians. All the retinue were well and appropriately dressed.

The King of the Dark Water, whose name was Suliken Rouah, treated the travellers with kingly munificence, presenting them with a jar of fine honey, two thousand cowries in money, and a large quantity of goora nuts, a description of food highly esteemed in Africa. He was a man of venerable and commanding appearance, and by reason of his wealth and power was no doubt entitled to the importance to which he laid claim.

The Landers at this stage of their journey exchanged their two canoes for one, and once more embarked on the river. They had sailed about thirty miles when they came upon a perfect swarm of hippopotami, which rose on all sides of the canoe, plunging, splashing, and snorting, and placing the frail vessel in great danger. A shot or two was fired at the great brutes, but only with the result of summoning a fresh horde up from the depths of the river and out of the neighbouring marshes. The natives in the canoe became terror-struck; and to add to the panic, a violent thunderstorm, succeeded by dense darkness, only illumined by occasional lightning flashes, burst suddenly over the heads of the party. The rowers pulled as for life, however, and after some hard rowing the swarm of hippopotami was left behind, and a little fishing village was reached, where the voyagers very gladly landed.

On October 19th Egga was reached, a town of great extent, in the centre of a fertile and fruitful region. Here the Englishmen were kindly enough treated by the aged king, a good-natured and gay-hearted old man, who bore a long tale of years with astonishing vigour and lightness of spirit. For the delectation of his guests, and also no doubt to display his unabated activity, the merry old chief performed a *pas seul* in their presence with surprising agility and nimbleness, until he seemed literally to " frisk beneath the burden" of his years.

After leaving Egga, the next place at which the Landers camped was Kacunda. About this point in its course the Niger changes its direction to south-south-west; and forty miles farther on it is joined by the Ishadda, by the influx of which the width of the main river is increased to between three and four miles.

By the end of October Damugoo was reached, where the Landers were very well received by the chief, who provided them with a canoe and a crew to conduct them to the coast. Shortly after leaving Damugoo the expedition had an unexpected encounter with a party of hostile natives near a large market town called Kirree. A fleet of canoes were observed moored by the banks of the river—of large size, and having flags flying from bamboo poles. No notice was taken of these canoes, but a little while afterwards the voyagers beheld a number of them coming up the river full of men, and decorated with flags. The travellers were allowing themselves to enjoy the lively and pleasing appearance presented by this native flotilla, when their feelings of gratification were quickly changed by the sudden warlike demonstrations of the advancing canoes.

A large canoe was quickly alongside that of the travellers, and with marvellous rapidity the whole of their property was transferred from one boat to the other. This unceremonious treatment was altogether too much for the temper of the Englishmen, and despite the enormous odds against them they began to show fight. Richard Lander, taking deliberate aim with his musket at the leader of the savages, a tall brawny fellow, would the next moment have sent a bullet through his body had not the weapon been wrested from his grasp by three more of the black men. Then Lander seized hold of another man, while Pascoe, the guide, with a well-aimed blow of his paddle, sent an opponent reeling backward into the canoe.

Daunted by the determined resistance of the white men, the men in the canoes made no further attack upon them. But the Landers had now lost everything;—clothes, medicine-chest, four guns (including that of Mr. Park); four cutlasses, two pistols, a number of very fine elephants' tusks (a present from the kings of Wowou and Boussa); a quantity of leopard skins, ostrich feathers, cowries, and other valuables; and finally, what was as serious a loss as any, the greater part of Richard Lander's journal.

In these disastrous circumstances the travellers determined to land at a town called Kirree, where, having reported the whole proceedings, they were informed that their case would be taken into consideration by the chief men. The Englishmen found friends at Kirree ready to sympathize with and aid them, and a palaver having been held, the outcome of the matter was, that the offenders, the robbers who had so shamelessly plundered the white men, were punished, and a part of their stolen property was recovered by the travellers. On the whole, this was perhaps the most threatening and disastrous episode in the journey; for not only had the Landers suffered serious loss of property, but had been in instant peril of their lives.

The voyagers arrived next at Eboe. Shortly before reaching the town they passed through a vast sheet of water like a lake, with low, swampy margin, thickly clothed with palm-trees. Here a considerable river, forming an important tributary of the Niger, flowed westward, while another took a south-easterly direction.

At Eboe the Landers were detained by King Obie, who, seeing an opportunity of obtaining a valuable ransom, was determined not to let it escape him. He required a present of English goods equivalent in value to twenty slaves. The brothers were both amazed and disconcerted by the amount of this demand, being entirely without hope of satisfying it. The prospect before them was gloomy in the extreme —indefinite detention at Eboe; but from their critical situation they were at length released by the intervention of King Boy of Brass Town, who promised to pay the sum demanded by King Obie, and to conduct the travellers safely to the end of their journey, if he was guaranteed a present equal to fifteen slaves, and the addition of a cask of rum on the arrival of the Englishmen at the coast. To this compact of King Boy the Landers very gladly agreed, and the travellers departed from Eboe conducted by King Boy.

At Brass Town the travellers were witnesses of a curious fetich ceremony. The priests began their operations by chalking King Boy from head to foot with circles, lines, and various fantastic devices, that so completely disguised his majesty that he was scarcely recognizable. Then having been disrobed of his usual dress, a small silk handkerchief was bound about his waist, while on his head was placed a close-fitting cap, decorated with the white and black feathers of a buzzard. When the king had taken in his hands two large chalked spears, his *ensemble* was as wild and strange as it was grotesque. His retinue were then similarly operated on, and finally the fetich priests themselves.

John Lander remained behind at Brass Town, while Richard proceeded to the coast. The English brig *Thomas* was lying at anchor in the Nun, a branch of the Niger, and Richard Lander immediately laid his position before the commander, Captain Lake, little doubting but that he would furnish means whereby King Boy's claims would be satisfied. In this hope he was grievously disappointed, Captain Lake showing a want of sympathy with the brothers in their strait for which it is difficult to account. He absolutely refused to advance the sum due to King Boy for his services; and Richard and John Lander, the latter of whom had now arrived from Brass Town, were obliged to depart in the brig, leaving King Boy in bitterness and dejection of spirit at not having received his promised reward. Nothing which the travellers could say availed to assure the chief that sooner or later he would receive the whole sum due to him; but on the return of the Landers to England, King Boy was paid his debt in full and with interest.

The travellers reached home on the 10th of June 1831. The success of their expedition was complete and indisputable, and the brothers Lander received from their countrymen the full measure of honours which they had so fairly earned. They had solved the problem of African exploration which had baffled so many previous travellers as courageous and enterprising but less fortunate than they, and had supplied the last link to the chain necessary to complete our knowledge of the Niger.

The journey of the Landers was far from being an easy and successful one throughout. In a rapid sketch of the expedition such as the foregoing, the many difficulties of the journey—the almost daily hardship, the sickness, the weariness, the disappointments, the frequent dejection and loneliness of spirit inseparable from African travel, all of which are rather matter of detail—do not fully appear. But a perusal of the travellers' journal itself reveals the innumerable obstacles with which the two brothers had to contend, and which only great fortitude, judgment, patience, and tact could have overcome. The written account of the expedition comprises a part of the journal of each of the brothers, and is written in a lively and interesting style, that portion contributed by John Lander, who had received a better education, and possessed greater literary facility than his elder brother, being especially marked by a fertile fancy and a power of vivid description.

Richard Lander was to take part in yet one other

African expedition. A scheme having been set on foot by a number of Liverpool merchants, whereby they hoped that commercial relations might be established with the natives along the banks of the Niger, two steamboats were fitted out—the *Quorra* and the *Alburkah*. The services of Richard Lander as leader of the enterprise were accepted. Messrs. Laird and Oldfield were second in command, and a strong party of other Europeans completed the expedition, which left England in July 1832.

The narrative of the voyage of the *Quorra* and the *Alburkah*, as told by Messrs. Laird and Oldfield, is full of interest. The expedition halted at many of the places visited by the Landers and other travellers, and had negotiations with several of the native chiefs already mentioned in these pages. Among the most interesting episodes in the voyage was an interview with King Obie, whose name the reader will recall in connection with the homeward journey of the Landers. In that instance the African chief had displayed a considerable degree of extortion as regards the value of the present which he demanded from the travellers, but in his dealings with the present mission he showed himself extremely conciliatory and amiable.

King Obie met the English party, richly arrayed in scarlet cloth, and adorned with massive coral chains, bracelets, and other ornaments, amounting in value to nearly one hundred pounds. Having shaken hands with Mr. Lander and Mr. Laird with great cordiality, he placed one on each side of his throne. The Englishmen were surprised at the pleasant and "gentlemanly" manner of King Obie; the latter epithet being most fairly applicable to the chief's whole conduct towards the travellers, for it was uniformly considerate and generous both in good and evil fortune.

The English party received from King Obie a present of a fine bullock, five goats, and three hundred yams. On the following morning a pleasing proof of the regular industry of King Obie's subjects was witnessed. At sunrise a large number of canoes of all sizes left the town, to collect palm oil, yams, and other commodities of the country; and towards evening the fleet—in number not less than a hundred and fifty—were seen dropping down the river again, laden with their cargoes of yams, bananas, and gourds full of palm oil.

On that day King Obie paid a visit to Mr. Lander on the *Alburkah*. His escort consisted of seven large war-canoes filled with rowers. Having dined with Mr. Lander, the chief remained some hours on board the vessel, and finally took his leave under a royal salute. He was escorted home by two of the sailors, whom he entertained at his own house with palm oil and roasted yams. This cordiality and good-fellowship were not confined to the king; all his subjects vied in their attentions to the members of the expedition.

KING OBIE'S VISIT TO THE "ALBURKAH."

As a commercial enterprise this mission—the last which we are to consider—proved a failure. The attempt to establish a trade intercourse with Central Africa came to nothing. Yet the expedition was not without results; the most important of which was, that it proved beyond a doubt that the mighty stream of the Niger was navigable for purposes of commerce from its mouth as far as Boussa.

Our rapid survey of African discovery in one important direction has, we trust, proved how deeply interesting is the whole subject of African exploration. Since the date of the formation of the African Association the world's interest in the "Dark Continent" has continued to grow and deepen, down to the present day. This interest is undoubtedly a healthy and natural one—it is an interest in the spread of knowledge, of civilization, and of Christianity. The vast African continent has year by year grown a little less "dark;" and as nation by nation and tribe by tribe of its dusky millions are reclaimed from darkness and linked to the rest of the discovered world, it is to emerge, we may surely hope, into the light of civilization, and finally of Christianity.

Our narrative has shown how many noble and gallant lives have been spent and lost in one field of African exploration; and to these must be added all those lost in other directions of the same work. But who shall say they have been lives vainly sacrificed?

Are they not all to be reckoned rather as parts of that vicarious sacrifice without which, it would seem, the progress of the world cannot subsist?

Even this brief narrative has, we think, furnished abundant proof of how capable the negro race is of humanizing influences; and the story of African discovery generally bears witness to the same fact. From Park to Moffat, and from Moffat to Stanley, the journals of every African traveller contain testimony more or less ample and conclusive to the truth of our statement. In these pages we have seen the African native sometimes fickle and inconstant, wily and rapacious; but we have seen him far more often gentle and faithful, warm-hearted and compassionate. We recall Park, again and again ministered to in hunger, nakedness, and sickness, with tender and pitying care; the brothers Lander, helped and cheered on their journey by many a deed of gentleness or of generosity; we think of Livingstone, spending years in the heart of the African wilderness, a solitary and lonely white man, without a single comrade of his own race to share his exile, but tended by his dark-skinned companions with the most watchful solicitude, loved and reverenced in life as a father and a teacher, and mourned in death with a sorrow at once too simple and too deep to be doubted; we remember Stanley in his adventurous and perilous journey testifying again and again that never had he known more faithful and devoted comradeship than that which he received from his negro companions;—and recalling these and a hundred kindred instances, the unprejudiced and candid mind must acknowledge that the negro character is capable of a high degree of affection, of gentleness, of self-sacrifice, devotion, and nobility.

Since the attention of England was first turned to the subject of African exploration much time and money and life has been spent in the work; but who, we repeat, will choose to say that either the time or the money or even the life has been wasted, if by their loss Africa is now emerging from the darkness of heathendom and savagery into the light of civilization, gentleness, and truth?

Volunteers for the work of African discovery have never failed—they are as promptly forthcoming now as they ever were; and almost every year witnesses some fresh and splendid achievement in this field of geographical enterprise. The records of African exploration furnish examples of courage and endurance, of patience, self-discipline, and self-sacrifice, that rise to the highest heroism: hardship, disaster, and death itself have never dismayed the African pioneer. When the last hero has ended his career only in a grave in the wilderness, a successor has never been wanting to tread in the same path. The torch has been passed on from one victorious or from one dying hand to another—the line has never been entirely broken; as one has fallen, another has been immediately at hand to fill up the breach—

> "Each stepping where his comrade stood
> The instant that he fell."

CHAPTER V.

EXPLORATION OF THE NIGER AND BENUEH BY M. ADOLPHE BURDO.

HAVING thus surveyed exploration in Western Africa in the past, we purpose giving the reader an idea of what has been done in the same direction in recent times. With this object in view, we cannot do better than present a brief summary of the travels of M. Adolphe Burdo, one of the latest explorers of the Niger and the regions watered by it.

M. Burdo left France in April 1878, and having arrived at Sierra Leone, proceeded thence to Bonny, situated in the delta of the Niger. The unhealthy climate of this region renders it impossible for the European inhabitants to live on the land. Resort is had, therefore, to hulks moored at the mouths of the rivers, which serve both as dwelling-houses and for purposes of commerce. The present king of Bonny, George Peppel, deserves a word of mention. He passed the early years of his life in England, and, in the midst of a still semi-savage and heathen race, comports himself in most respects like a European. Some time ago the English nation presented him with a small steamer, aided by which the king carries on a brisk trade in palm oil.

At Bonny M. Burdo was told that it would be impossible to reach the Niger from that point. He therefore proceeded to Brass, and there began his preparations for his voyage on the great river by procuring a half-decked canoe and engaging twelve Kroomen to man it. In a little while all was ready for the start, and the canoe was afloat on one of the innumerable creeks which form the delta of the Niger.

The utter solitude and gloom which reign over this portion of the Niger, exert a most depressing influence on the traveller beginning his long voyage. Destitute alike of flower or grass as well as of almost all animal life, the only sound that breaks the tomb-like silence is the mournful swaying of the slimy-branched aquatic trees from which here and there long snakes may be seen trailing.

The progress made by the party was slow and unsatisfactory. Again and again their course was completely arrested by impenetrable barriers of mangroves. The fresh provisions became exhausted, and no human habitations were visible on the banks. On the fourth day from the start, the conclusion forced itself upon M. Burdo that he had lost his way in this dreary maze of creeks and mangrove swamps. Despondency and terror now took possession of the Kroomen, and they abandoned their rowing. It was with the greatest difficulty that M. Burdo succeeded in reanimating their drooping spirits, and inspiring them with sufficient energy to renew their labours.

After a time the channel in which the canoe was sailing widened, and M. Burdo was in hopes that his difficulties were so far over, and that his further progress would be unimpeded. But he soon discovered that the creek, instead of leading in the direction of the Niger, was evidently bearing them towards the sea, and presently the water became quite salt.

Darkness fell: the channel became wider and wider, and presently a light was descried on the bank. The canoe was steered for the welcome beacon, but the current now became so strong that the voyagers were borne past the light and hurried rapidly towards the open ocean.

A noise as of breaking surf was now heard, and a white line was visible straight ahead. A new danger threatened the party. The white line could only be the surf dashing against the reefs that barred the mouth of the river. Anchor was at once cast, and the canoe brought up with so sudden a shock as almost to break the cable.

The Kroomen slept, but M. Burdo's anxiety was too great to admit of slumber. The cable might break at any moment, and the canoe be hurried to instant destruction. By morning, however, the violence of the current had lessened, for the tide had turned. A factory was observed on the bank of the river, and towards it the canoe was at once steered. The station at which the party now landed was Akassa, and the stream which had come so near to being the destruction of the explorers was the Nun, which M. Burdo had been especially anxious to avoid on account of the impetuosity of its current.

Akassa is destined to be a place of importance, should the Niger and Benueh one day be opened to the European trader, for it would probably then become the point of union between the factories on these rivers and the countries of Europe.

From Akassa M. Burdo and his party were conveyed by the steamer of the African Company to Onitsha, up the broad and rapid stream of the Nun. Emerging from this river, the Niger itself was at last gained, and the scenery at once entirely changed its character. The sombre maze of creeks and the interminable mangrove swamps which, as has been indicated, characterize the delta, gave place to a broad and noble river, its banks clothed with all the luxuriance of African vegetation. Cocoa-nut, banana, and cotton trees waved their branches against the sky, and birds of rainbow plumage fluttered amid the thick leafage, while ever and again a village peeped out from behind its green bower.

En route to Onitsha, Aboh was stopped at, the largest town in the district, and commercially one of the most active. An energetic and warlike race, the natives of Aboh are extremely jealous of the white man. They are at incessant feud with the neighbouring tribes, pass their lives chiefly on the water, and, in short, are little else than a race of pirates.

Onitsha lies on the left bank of the Niger, in latitude 6° 8′ north. Taking leave of the little steamer and its captain, M. Burdo now disembarked. At this point two of his followers deserted, and two others having proved equally faithless at Akassa, the expedition was reduced to eight men exclusive of the leader.

It was market-day when M. Burdo arrived at Onitsha, and the river was thronged with canoes, while the banks were lined with a motley and excited crowd of traders from the town itself and from the neighbouring tribes. The market-place presented a curious sight. Women offered their wares for sale, consisting chiefly of palm oil and ivory, together with beads, calicoes, and gin or rum. The men walked in and out among the saleswomen and made their purchases, cowries being the medium of exchange. A great diversity of race was to be noticed among the negroes, and their colour varied from ebony to copper.

The king of Onitsha received M. Burdo with signal marks of friendliness, and with all the pomp he could command. He was seated in the royal hut on a carpet of red velvet, dressed in a green mantle, and on his head a large hat of leaves decorated with a plume of white feathers. He was surrounded by a large suite of attendants.

To the words of salutation and congratulation addressed to him by M. Burdo the king returned a gracious reply, and then offered the stranger palm wine and *kolas*, a sort of almonds, red and of a bitter taste. M. Burdo was then requested to be seated— a conspicuous mark of favour on the negro monarch's part, as no one of his own people is permitted to sit in his presence.

The customary exchange of presents followed, and the king seemed well contented with the white man's gift—a parcel of calicoes, with bead-strings, mirrors, and a knife. M. Burdo received from his host in return a welcome addition to his stock of provisions, in the shape of fowls, bananas, a jar of palm wine, and a whole ox.

M. Burdo found that the women of Onitsha occupy a somewhat less degraded position than is the case among most negro tribes. Commercial negotiations are commonly intrusted to them, and in this department they display a large amount of shrewdness. They follow their husbands to battle, and play the part of *vivandières* with both courage and gentleness.

At Onitsha M. Burdo engaged seventeen natives as rowers, and the expedition now consisted of two canoes. At Atane the main stream of the Niger was quitted for a while, and a creek entered traversing the Obotshi country. Swarms of hippopotami were discovered in this stream, one of which M. Burdo succeeded in killing. When night approaches, these animals come up out of the water to feed on the long grass on the banks. All night they browse on these pastures, and at daybreak again seek the river-bed.

The next halt was made at Accre, where M. Burdo found the king engaged in fêting a neighbouring prince. The white man was invited to witness the rejoicings, and conducted to the king's presence. The prince of Accre and his friend the King Oputa both rose at the white man's approach and gave him a cordial welcome. King Oputa, a young man with a singularly grave and even melancholy cast of countenance for a negro, could understand a few words of English.

The *fête* was now continued with much uproar of fifes and tom-toms. Dance followed dance, while the public singers chanted the praises of the two kings, mingling with these complimentary extemporized verses in honour of the white man.

It was arranged that M. Burdo should continue his journey in company with King Oputa and his retinue, and having warmly thanked the king of Accre for his kind reception, the traveller once more embarked. M. Burdo parted from King Oputa at a point where the creek forked, the traveller striking northward, the king taking a westerly course towards the Niger.

The territory which the expedition now entered is called Esuama-Ebo, a district of large extent. The religion of the natives is almost pure idolatry; but some slight traces of Judaism may be discovered in it—a circumstance which seems to indicate that some stray wanderers of the Hebrew race must long ago have found their way to these regions, and in the gradual course of time become assimilated to the natives both in appearance and customs, leavening the races around them, however, with a few of their own ideas. Thus the people of Ebo believe in a God, Orissa or Tshuku, who is supreme and omnipotent; as well as in an evil spirit corresponding to Satan, whom they name Kamallo, or Igwik-Alla. When it is explained that *Igwik* means "one who has fallen from a place of honour," and that *Alla* denotes "earth," the parallel between *Igwik-Alla* and the fallen angel of the Scriptures may be readily recognized.

As the Jews had their sacred city Jerusalem, so the people of Ebo have their holy city Aro, to which they make many pilgrimages, as the followers of the Prophet do to Mecca.

Quitting Ebo, M. Burdo faced north-east, and presently reached N'Teja, which he found in a state of great excitement consequent on the king having declared war with his neighbours the Ogidis. King

Ogene received the white man favourably enough, but absolutely forbade him to advance further into his territories. He promised, however, to show M. Burdo another route by which the Niger might be reached. The apparent reason for this course of action on the king's part was that he feared that the white man's presence among his enemies, the Ogidis, might bring with it the favour of the Great Spirit. After witnessing a curious religious rite, by which King Ogene sought to propitiate the god Tshuku in favour of his arms, M. Burdo departed in a northerly direction towards Imam.

The natives of Ebo are a fierce and war-loving people. Giving no quarter and seeking none, they make neither slaves nor prisoners, but put all captives to death without mercy. They carry out the stern old code, "an eye for an eye, and a tooth for a tooth," to the letter. If a man murders another, the victim's relatives pursue the murderer to the death; and if the assassin finally escapes, some one of his relatives suffers death in his stead, and thus justice is appeased.

The negroes regard life as falling into four epochs— namely, infancy; youth, when a person must look after himself; manhood, when a man may take a wife; and old age, when he is looked upon as little better than a burden to his friends and the state. It must in justice be stated, however, that a great difference in regard to this last custom exists among different tribes. Some of the native races along the Niger pay all due respect to their old men, seeking their counsel both in peace and war.

A man's wives in negro-land are usually in proportion to his fortune. The wife becomes to all intents a slave; and so far from looking with a jealous eye upon a fresh arrival in the seraglio, she welcomes the new-comer as a sharer in the household work and drudgery.

On the second day after leaving the country of the Ogidis the expedition had a sharp encounter with hostile natives, about thirty in number. M. Burdo's followers behaved well, and succeeded in routing their assailants; but not before one—the bravest of the band—paid forfeit with his life. This was "Go-fast," one of the trustiest of M. Burdo's escort, who fell pierced by an arrow. Everything possible was done for the wounded man, but poor Go-fast subsequently died of his hurt.

On the day following this encounter and catastrophe the party reached the territory of Annam, a fertile region, rich in palm-trees, yams, and bananas. M. Burdo was interested in the method of fishing adopted by the natives of this district, which is curious and ingenious.

Wooden constructions, resembling rude sentry-boxes, supported on poles, are set up in mid-stream. In these the fishermen take their station, with a large oblong net made of fibre, to which is secured a basket. This net, with the basket depending from the middle, the fisherman lowers by a rope into the water. Two comrades, seated in a canoe near the bank, narrowly watch the casting of the net, and as soon as it is drawn up they approach and receive the catch, whatever it may be. Then the net is again lowered, and so *da capo*. Great quantities of fish are frequently taken by this method.

M. Burdo was now told that the great river Osimirin—the name which the natives of these parts give to the Niger—was near at hand; and presently the expedition reached Ogbekin, the capital of King Oputa's country, situated on a creek of the Niger, in 6° 25′ north latitude.

The traveller was met by King Oputa and a large following, who conducted him to the village, entertained him with palm wine, bananas, and kolas, and furnished him with a hut for himself.

M. Burdo now paid off some of his men whose term of service had expired, and was immediately provided with another canoe and more men by King Oputa.

During his stay at Ogbekin M. Burdo witnessed the festival of the *Waye*, held to signalize the sprouting of the yam crop, and an important ceremony among the natives. The whole tribe was gathered together about the royal huts, and proceeded thence to a large bombax-tree. The priest then took a number of newly-gathered yams, some kola nuts, and fresh fish, which had been brought by the chiefs as an offering. The yams having been sliced up by the priest, the king received and ate a piece, and was followed in like manner by his chiefs in turn, each first pronouncing the words, "Thanks be to Tshuka, who permits me to eat the waye." The religious part of the rite being performed, the ceremony winds up with a merry-making.

A rite of a very different kind obtains among the Ogbekin tribes, which the influence of Christianity has not yet touched in any degree. This is the yearly ceremony of expiation, performed to atone both for the sins of the king and the people.

Two young girls, chosen generally from hostile tribes, having been stripped of all clothing, are decked out by the priests in a fantastic garb of leaves, flowers, and tinsel. They are then led out and exposed to the violence of the mob, who assail them with vituperation of every description, shouting, "Arroyé, arroyé" (Accursed, accursed). Finally the victims are put to death. Among some tribes it is the custom to take the victim in a canoe into the middle of the river, and, fastening a heavy weight to her person, drown her.

This is a very ancient and deep-rooted custom, and by its due observance it is believed that whatever crimes may have been committed by the king and his people during the year are washed out by the blood of the sacrifice. May the time be hastened when the spread of civilization and the softening power of Christianity shall end this cruel and frightful barbarism.

King Oputa, the grave and melancholy, treated M. Burdo with great hospitality, even to the extent of offering him one of the prettiest and most favourite of his wives. The black monarch hardly concealed his surprise at his guest declining this gift, and M. Burdo had some difficulty in making his host comprehend the nature of the tie between husband and wife among Europeans. The king could only account for a white man having but one wife on the score of poverty; in fact, it was clear that neither he nor his wives quite believed M. Burdo's statements in regard to the faithfulness of the white man to his wife, receiving them with much good-humoured but incredulous laughter.

Oputa showed much regret at parting from M. Burdo, who proceeded from Ogbekin to Asaba, situated 6° 11′ north. Asaba, in its external aspect, was one of the most curious towns visited by the traveller. A temple stood in the centre of the town, adorned with the most grotesque idols, one of these representing a huge figure of a mother with new-born children beside her. The walls of the temple were decorated with rude frescoes of wild beasts of strange and unknown shapes.

M. Burdo's stay at Asaba was short, and he was soon once more on the river, passing Abijaga on the left bank, the Lander islands, and the Ojona islands. At Ibbah, in latitude 7° 6′ north, he halted. Ibbah is a stronghold of Islamism, though situated in negro-land; and the language spoken by the people is *Houssa*, which very nearly resembles Arabic. The scenery on quitting Ibbah is of great beauty and grandeur. The banks of the river rise on either side to a vast height —sheer walls of granite; and through these, gazing upward, the voyager beholds the strip of sky, bright blue by day, purple and set with stars at night; while the rushing of the river through the rocky gorge is the only sound that breaks the silence and deep calm of the scene.

Not long after leaving Ibbah a great misfortune befell the traveller—namely, the desertion of the whole of his men with the exception of three. The cause of this unfaithfulness, probably, was fear on the part of the men at the prospect of the unknown Benueh—the final goal of the expedition.

M. Burdo's situation was now critical enough, but he extorted a promise from his three remaining Kroomen to remain faithful. This oath of allegiance the three men took an early opportunity of breaking, and the traveller was left absolutely alone!

With forebodings of the darkest colour M. Burdo pursued his solitary way in his canoe, and having anchored at dawn near a village, gathered together his chattels, and examined his arms, prepared for the worst that might happen in the shape of hostile reception on the part of the villagers.

Presently he beheld a group of people, who answered his signs by shouting and laughter. This reception was, at best, somewhat doubtful; but the traveller had nothing for it but to put a bold face on matters. Displaying a strip of calico in one hand and a bead necklace in the other, he stood up in the canoe and made signs to the negroes that he wished some of them to row for him. First one and then another got into the boat, until M. Burdo had a crew of four; and thus assisted in the rowing, in the space of half an hour the traveller had reached the village of Lokoja. Here he was met by a large crowd, who, to his no small surprise, seemed to be expecting his arrival. But his astonishment increased tenfold when on landing he was thus accosted in English by a negro, dressed in a jacket and trowsers :—

"This morning the Bishop of the Niger was informed by a fisherman that there was a white man in these parts. He has sent me to you to ask if you are in need of help : he places his house at your disposal and offers you hospitality."

Such a greeting brought M. Burdo no less delight than astonishment; for it meant for him succour and sympathy when he most needed them. He was now conducted to the mission-station, which is situated at the foot of Mount Patuh, near Lokoja. The Bishop of the Niger, Samuel Ajai Crowther, was an old man with white hair, dressed in a long black coat and trowsers to match. He received M. Burdo most cordially, and the two had much to tell each other. The bishop strongly urged the traveller not to attempt the Benueh in a canoe, on account of its rapid current. He advised instead that M. Burdo should ascend the river in the small steamer *Henry Venn*, the property of the Church Missionary Society. The traveller, of course, at once saw the reason of this, and agreed to the bishop's suggestion.

Bishop Crowther is stationed at Lokoja during the rainy season only; for the remainder of the year he lives at Lagos on the coast. The natives of Lokoja belong for the most part to the Mohammedan faith, and Christianity has not as yet made much headway among them. A certain amount of civilized industry obtains in the village, and M. Burdo saw a small forge, a few cloth-looms, and a dye-vat.

During his stay at Lokoja, M. Burdo received from Bishop Crowther a narrative of the chief events of his life—a recital full of interest. He was born on the Benueh, but remembered little or nothing of his childhood. During an attack on his native village, when he was about nine years old, he saw his father killed before his eyes. He hung about his mother, but was carried off by the enemy. For a year he suffered extreme hardships at the hands of his captors, and was finally sold to Portuguese slave-dealers.

The boy was shipped in company with a number of others in a vessel with a double deck, so constructed that at short notice the whole cargo could be let down into the sea, in the event of the ship being boarded by an English or French cruiser. In her passage from Old Calabar the ship was chased by an English sloop, captured and boarded. In the confusion which ensued on board the slave-ship, the boy contrived to conceal himself among some salt-bags, and thus escaped. The captain of the English cruiser had his sympathy awakened by the lad's case, landed him at Sierra Leone, and had him put to school. Subsequently he proceeded to London, made excellent progress in his studies, and was finally ordained and sent to the African mission field.

Crowther made a very zealous and successful missionary; and his remarkable fitness for the work was recognized by his being made a bishop by the Archbishop of Canterbury in 1864, the region of the Upper Niger being appointed him as his diocese.

One day, when Bishop Crowther was preaching in a large village, suddenly an aged woman rushed from the crowd and seized the preacher round the neck, crying, "My son! my son!" It was his mother. The men who had slain Crowther's father had not thought it worth their while to take the mother, and she had escaped. For nearly thirty years she had been in search of her son, wandering from tribe to tribe, and had at last found him thus—a bishop! She passed the remainder of her life in peace and comfort, gently tended to her latest days by her son. Such is the story of Samuel Ajai Crowther.

M. Burdo embarked on the little steamer *Henry Venn* in company with Bishop Crowther and Mr. J. Ashcroft, agent of one of the missionary societies. After leaving Lokoja, Duck Island and Oromay were passed, and presently the mouth of the Benueh was entered. The negroes give the name of Neehu, or Leehu, to this river; the Mussulmans call it Baiki N'Ruwa—that is, White Water; while the Niger they call Fari N'Ruwa, or Black Water.

Igbegbe, a village of evil notoriety for its traffic in slaves, is situated at the junction of the two rivers. As you ascend the Benueh, or Schadda, navigation is rendered difficult and dangerous by the numerous sandbanks, and the captain of the *Henry Venn* had constantly to take soundings, besides keeping the most vigilant look-out ahead. Even thus, the steamer once ran aground near the Harriet Islands; but her paddle-wheels being reversed, she was not long in being again free. Large numbers of alligators were seen on the sandbanks, basking in the sun, with gaping jaws and hideous gleaming teeth.

On the following day Imaha was reached, situated on a small creek about half a mile from the main river. The king of Imaha was absent from his capital, engaged in laying siege to Amara, higher up the river. The party therefore remained only one day here, and then proceeded towards Amara, the steamer casting anchor within a short distance of the besieged town. Two canoes came alongside, and a chief, seated in one of them, announced to the strangers that King Kpanaki was willing to see them. It was Bishop Crowther's intention to establish, if possible, a mission among King Kpanaki's subjects.

On reaching the king's camp, M. Burdo was surprised at the degree of order and military discipline maintained among the troops, who were all drawn up in regular battalions according to the several tribes of which the army was composed. A band of natives, playing on tom-toms, drums, and bamboo fifes, conducted the strangers to the king's presence, who received them seated on a sort of rude throne, constructed of mat-work supported on stakes. Wooden seats were placed for the strangers.

King Kpanaki was between thirty and forty years old, of a pure negro type, with a severe expression of face. On his head he wore a leather cap surmounted by a plume of white feathers, numerous rings adorned his fingers, and about his waist was wound a broad band of scarlet cloth.

Bishop Crowther stated the object of his visit, telling the king that his (Kpanaki's) father had expressed a wish to see the Christian religion introduced among his people. The bishop then went on to say that the God of the Christians forbade war such as Kpanaki was now carrying on with his neighbours. To this the king answered, that he desired to respect his father's wishes, but that he could not discontinue the war.

M. Burdo then told of the desire on the part of Europeans to trade with the king, to exchange the manufactures of England and France — clothes, weapons, iron, and copper—for the products of Africa, —for ivory, gold, and palm oil; adding that such a commerce could not be initiated with a people immersed in war and rapine.

Then King Kpanaki proposed to call his chiefs together to take into consideration the question of making peace with the foe. For a little it seemed likely that peaceful counsels might prevail, when suddenly a great uproar was heard in the camp, in the midst of which a man entered unbidden the hut in which this scene was being enacted.

The new-comer was N'Dako, the captain of the king of Bida—a man notorious for his boldness, his activity in the slave-trade, and his hatred of white men. His arrival put an entirely altered complexion on matters, and rendered the position of M. Burdo,

Mr. Ashcroft, and Bishop Crowther extremely critical. N'Dako had soon won over the king to his way of thinking, and the strangers were told that they must at once depart from the camp and give up all thought of penetrating further into King Kpanaki's territory. Hostile looks now greeted the strangers on all sides, outside the uproar increased, and swords were drawn and flashed threateningly. M. Burdo deemed that not a moment was to be lost in escaping, and he made a way for himself and his companions through the mob of soldiers, who seemed more than half ready to fall upon the strangers. But they had soon reached the river-bank, and were presently again seated in their canoe. Meanwhile King Kpanaki was preparing to lead his soldiers to the sacking of Amara.

M. Burdo now parted from Bishop Crowther, the latter returning in the steamer to the Niger. The parting was with mutual regret, for M. Burdo had conceived for the black bishop a regard and respect equally sincere. Bishop Crowther placed in the traveller's hands a letter for the King of the Belgians, which in due course was faithfully delivered.

The traveller now pursued his journey accompanied by one follower only—the faithful Ben Ali—guide and interpreter. His resources were coming to an end, but he was resolved to travel on as long as they held out.

The sources of the river Benueh still await a discoverer, and the complete and final survey of this mysterious stream will probably supply a key to not a few problems of African exploration.

On the right side of the Benueh, near its confluence with the Niger, lies the country of Igbira-Panda, which marches with Oketa. Next, following the same bank of the river, comes Bassa, then Egy, Doma, and Dotshi, which reaches to the Murchison Mountains. Akpoto lies on the left bank; next Agadumo, Mitshi, Anufo, and Karorofan. Then the Hamaruwa country begins, occupying both banks of the river. Next comes Adamawa, with its capital, Yola.

The Mussulman power has a strong hold on the Benueh and Upper Niger territory. Its chief centre is Sokoto, situated on a tributary of the Niger— the river Fadam. The followers of Mohammed, led by the fierce chief Fodje, invaded this region, and making terrible havoc among the natives, took possession of the country intermediate between Soudan and the Benueh. It is extremely doubtful whether the Mussulman faith, which has been thus grafted on, or in many cases has superseded, the idolatry of the original possessors of the land, will do anything to further civilization and a gentler life in Central Africa. The appearance upon the scene of the followers of the Prophet has as yet brought with it only rapine, conflagration, and increased slavery.

Among the people of Akpoto and Mitshi pure and

simple barbarism prevails. They are cannibals, idol-worshippers, and offerers of human sacrifices. Their religious ceremonies reveal one or two perverted traits of Judaism, among the rest circumcision. Two great spirits are worshipped and feared by them—the spirit of evil and the spirit of good; but the former is held in by far the greater awe. Serpents, alligators, and all animals hostile to man, personify to their minds the evil spirit; while trees, rivers, and stars are symbolical of the good spirit.

By the time M. Burdo had reached Luwo, he found that his resources were almost at an end. It was impossible to pursue his explorations further, for he had barely sufficient money, etc., to carry him back to the coast. At every village through which he had passed he had to pay toll in the shape of a gift to the king or chief. He resolved, therefore, to retrace his steps through the Akpoto country, and presently reached the river Okari, which the traveller judged to be identical with the Bonny. As his homeward journey continued, his difficulties increased. His provisions grew scantier and more scanty, the natives proved hostile and treacherous, fatigue and want of sleep weakened him in body and spirit, and it was with the greatest effort that he prevented himself from yielding to despair. Added to these various discouragements, he suffered severely from the bite of a snake, which caused such acute pain and numbness that he could only continue his journey at a very slow pace.

At length, to his great satisfaction, M. Burdo met his old friend King Oputa, on his way with a party of his people to conclude a treaty of peace with the king of Ogberi. The traveller accompanied his black friend to Ogberi, which was reached the same day. Zumbadi, the king, received the white man favourably, giving him a separate hut for his accommodation. Rest and the sense of relief from anxiety soon refreshed the traveller in mind and body.

During his stay at Ogberi, M. Burdo was compelled to be present at a human sacrifice—a sacred ceremony which it would have perhaps cost him his own life to have refused to witness. The ceremony was accompanied with a very carnival of hideous noises and barbaric dances, over which the moonlight shed a ghastly radiance, until the whole horrible and heart-sickening scene so impressed itself upon the white man's imagination that sleep fled from his eyes for that night.

The religion of the people of Ogberi is a sort of compromise between idolatry and Mohammedanism. They obey the laws of the Koran for the most part, but are in reality polytheists. In regard to industrial pursuits, cultivation is in a comparative state of advancement among them—yams, maize, bananas, the cassava and tobacco being grown; and palm and bamboo wine, together with a kind of beer, manufactured.

The natives of the Benueh region are for the most part very ill-favoured, the women among them being obese to the extent of deformity. They are an industrious people, on the whole, and work in copper with no small skill, while their pottery displays a degree of adornment that may be compared to Egyptian art of this description.

Quitting Ogberi, M. Burdo in six days reached Igbegbe, where the Niger and Benueh meet. Here he had an opportunity of studying the slave-market in full operation—"the saddest sight in the world." Men, women, and children were put up to auction and sold "like beasts of burden,"—the prices paid varying from four pounds to forty.

At Lokay, M. Burdo embarked on board the little steamer *Edgar*, and arriving at Lagos, took passage for Liverpool in the steamer *Roquelle*. When he landed in his native country—Belgium—he had been eight months on his travels; and during all that period, though he had had quite the usual share of hardship, privation, and suffering which falls to every traveller in Africa, he had never suffered seriously in health. A hostile climate, fatigue, fever, incessant anxiety, and a thousand minor worries, had left him physically unimpaired, and he returned to Europe with heartfelt gratitude to Heaven for safety and restoration.

CHAPTER VI.

CAPTAIN GALLIENI'S EXPEDITION TO THE UPPER NIGER.*

In the work of African exploration France has not been inactive, and among the expeditions projected by that nation that of Captain Gallieni must take rank as the most important, both in regard to the difficulties surmounted and the results obtained.

Captain Gallieni had recently returned from a journey of exploration to southern Senegambia, when Monsieur Briere de l'Isle, the governor of Senegal, unfolded to him a plan for penetrating the valley of the Upper Niger by way of the lofty mountain-pass extending between that great river and the Senegal. The main object of the expedition was to establish friendly relations with the native races partially made known to Europeans by the travels of Mungo Park, and to open up to the French frontier colonies of Mediné and Bakel an outlet to markets hitherto

---

* The following is an abstract of Captain Gallieni's own narrative, which appeared in "Le Tour du Monde."

abandoned to semi-savage tribes. All the territory which was to be traversed, extending from Mediné as far as the banks of the Niger, is under the nominal sovereignty of Amadou, king of Ségou.

Captain Gallieni chose for his companions in travel M. Pietri, a lieutenant of Marine Artillery; M. Valliere, a lieutenant of Marine Infantry; and MM. Tautain and Bayol, two young doctors—all men possessing special qualifications for the respective duties they were to perform.

Captain Gallieni, well knowing how readily the negro races are affected by showy spectacle, kept this point well in view in the equipment of his expedition. His escort was numerous and equipped at all points, and presented a *tout ensemble* well calculated to excite the wonder and admiration of the simple natives.

The month of January 1880 was employed in making all necessary provision for the journey. At St. Louis an immense stock of presents was laid in— the means of securing the good offices of the tribes. These comprised coloured stuffs of various sorts— white calicoes, blue guinea cloth, Indian scarves, gay-coloured handkerchiefs, gilt swords, silver-mounted guns, knives, mirrors, musical boxes, little electrical machines, etc. At Bakel the finishing touch was given to the preparations, every detail of which had been arranged with the care and minuteness so necessary to the success of an expedition of this sort.

On the 30th January a flag hoisted over the house of the governor gave the signal for the start. MM. Bayol, Pietri, and Valliere embarked on the steamboat *Dakar*, to which were attached the boats, and launches laden with the heavy freight which had to be transported as far as Bakel by water. Captain Gallieni himself and Dr. Tautain, who had been detained at St. Louis at the last moment, set out a little later on board the *Swan*, accompanied by the governor and his lieutenant. M. Briere de l'Isle had followed with the keenest interest all the preparations for the expedition, and now accompanied the travellers as far as Podor, as a last mark of the importance which he attached to the success of the mission.

It was with feelings of deep emotion that the travellers pressed for the last time the hands of their friends, whom some of them might perhaps never see again. But the thoughts of the explorers were ere long turned in other directions by the stir and bustle on board, by the cries of the negroes, and by the new scenes through which they were passing. On the right lay the country of the Trarzan Moors, and on the left the territory of the Ouoloff negroes.

Ouoloff is subject to the French government, and pays tribute to a considerable amount. The Trarzas, on the opposite bank of the river, are among the most turbulent of the Moorish tribes; but an important trade is carried on between them and the French at

Dagana—the Trarzas bartering their gums for guinea cloth, a cheap blue stuff, and other products of European manufacture. In the winter they quit the banks of the river—very much to the satisfaction of the black river tribes, who have frequently to suffer at the hands of these shameless robbers—return to the desert, and resume their wandering and adventurous life, in which war and pillage play the most important part.

The first important halt which M. Gallieni and his companions made along the river was at Dagana, situated on the banks of the Senegal, and almost entirely hidden among thick trees. From one end of the veranda of a house there appeared every now and then, as the travellers drew near, the black heads of pretty little monkeys, of a gray, green-coloured species, which abound in the forests of Fouta, and are a source of infinite amusement to the soldiers of the forts.

The town itself presented a lively sight. The traders, standing on the steps of their white, square-shaped houses, disputed eagerly with the Moors, whose black, flowing, uncombed hair gave them a strangely savage appearance. In the middle of the path camels reclined with long stretched-out legs, and regarded with startled eyes all that was going on around them. The *Dakar* only stopped long enough at Dagana to land some of its black passengers, and in a few minutes was again on its course for Podor, followed closely by the *Swan*.

Podor was reached on the evening of January 31. It was regarrisoned by the French with a strong force in 1854, in the face of the hostility of the Toucouleurs of Toro. The fort itself consists of two parallel streets, one of which, shady with fine trees, borders the Senegal. Behind rise the pointed roofs of the native villages of Podor and Tioffy.

On the 3rd of February, the governor, M. Briere de l'Isle, gave the mission their last instructions. "Go," he said. "Be energetic, be resolute. Forget the trials which await you, to remember only the interests of your country. You are about to initiate a grand undertaking, and I, for my part, shall use every endeavour to see that you are soon followed in the path which you will open up to civilization and the influence of the French nation. My good wishes and those of the whole colony go with you. God prosper your noble and patriotic efforts."

On the morning of the 4th, the voyagers re-embarked, on board the *Dakar*, which was to take them as far as the bank of the Mafou, at which point they parted with the steamer.

Among the inconveniences of Senegalese life, the greatest is the difficulty of communication, during a large part of the year, between the chief town of the colony and the settlements situated beyond Podor.

FRENCH EXPEDITION AGAINST THE TOUCOULEURS.

Page 161.

Steamboats cannot ascend further than the shallows of the Mafou, and recourse must be had to flat-bottomed boats, which often consume a whole month in reaching Mediné. Sometimes the black sailors who have charge of these craft land on the banks, fasten a long rope to the masts, and thus drag the boats along. Often, however, the thick vegetation of the river-banks renders this device impracticable, and branches and long poles have then to be used. Under conditions such as these it will easily be imagined how slow and monotonous progress becomes, especially when the numerous shallows and rapids which obstruct both the lower and upper Senegal are remembered.

Toro was now reached, one of the states annexed in a measure by the French from the powerful and turbulent confederation of Fouta. The hostility displayed by the Toucouleurs, and their predilection for plunder, obliged the French to make frequent expeditions against these wandering tribes. As one result of this policy, Toro became an independent state under the protectorate of the French, and is governed by a young chief, Amadou Abdoul, who is now almost a naturalized Frenchman, and who visited the Paris Exhibition of 1878.

The other bank of the river forms the boundary-line of the territory of the Brackna Moors, who carry on a brisk trade in gums with the fort at Podor.

The navigation was slow and difficult for some days. Owing to the thickly-wooded character of the banks, the boats could not be towed along by ropes secured to the masts. Captain Gallieni and his comrades relieved the tediousness of the journey by shooting at the alligators asleep on the surface of the stream. The huge creatures plunged suddenly beneath the water, leaving a thin stream of blood behind them, which sufficiently showed that some of the shots had not been without effect. On the summits of the banks black-headed monkeys and birds of many-coloured plumage fled at the approach of the travellers.

On the 9th, the villages of Cascas and Doungel were passed; and soon after, not without difficulty and much loss of time, the difficult passage of Djoulédiabé. Here, however, the banks being unwooded, the method of towing could again be put into practice.

The next halt was made at Saldé, where a stock of fresh provisions was laid in. Boussea was presently in sight—a place inhabited by the most unruly tribe of all the Toucouleur confederacy. Its chief, Abdoul Boubakar, surrounded by an energetic band of young warriors, living entirely by plunder, does his utmost to excite against the French the more peaceable villages situated along the river with whom that nation has commercial relations.

The river continued to be of imposing breadth. On

the Fouta side the banks are well wooded. As far as Matam many traces of cultivation were observed. On the 14th, Oréfondé, the capital of all the Toucouleur confederacy, was reached. Here are usually held the assemblies of fanatic Mussulmans, who combine against the French and their native *protégés*. These wild convocations result in little more than talk and uproar, and generally break up without arriving at any serious determination.

Plenty of hippopotami were now met with, the voyagers being made aware of their propinquity by loud snortings. They frequently rose up out of the river a few yards from the boats, which ran some risk of being swamped by them. Fire was opened upon these huge river-horses, but with not much result; for when wounded the creatures plunged immediately to the bottom of the river.

Notwithstanding the activity of the black sailors, Matam was not reached until the 18th. It is situated on the confines of Boussea and Damga, the last state of Fouta. Damga is a more populous region than any that had been crossed thus far. The inhabitants are a peaceable people, who desire nothing better than to be delivered from the continual raids of Abdoul Boubakar.

The vegetation now became more luxuriant and beautiful. Trees of various species abounded—palms of different varieties and tamarinds of great height and elegant form being especially numerous. The picturesque foliage of the trees, the hills and red-brown rocks which formed a background to the vegetation, and villages set more closely together, gave to the country a very bright and lively look, and made a pleasant relief to the eye after the long monotony of the forest.

On the morning of the 25th the expedition arrived at Tuabo, the residence of the *tunka* or chief of Guoy. A few hours later Bakel was in sight, recognizable by its high towers crowning the hills around the fort. Next the white and massive buildings were visible, and at four o'clock in the afternoon the voyagers cast anchor, happy to quit the narrow and difficult passage through which they had been passing for the last twenty days. The first stage of the voyage was accomplished, and the journey was henceforth to be a land one.

The fort of Bakel dates from the beginning of the century. It replaced the various factories formerly established in that region by the Indian Company, to prosecute the gold trade of Galam and Bambouk. It is at the present day a fine building, restored by the exertions of the governor, Briere de l'Isle, composed of two large wings connected by a smaller building. The officers' quarters are airy and commodious, while those of the men are equally comfortable and well arranged. In fact, nothing has been left undone to

GALLIENI'S EXPEDITION ON THE SENEGAL BETWEEN MATAM AND BAKEL.

Page 163.

minimise the discomforts of life in a country abounding in malarious marshes and hostile in every way to the health of European residents.

This station is the most important on the river, and carries on an active trade in gums, horses, gold, ostrich feathers, skins, etc. The commandant, M. Soyer, received the expedition with every mark of hospitality, and some time was spent by Captain Gallieni and his officers in reorganizing the large and somewhat heterogeneous forces—men, cattle, and baggage—under their command.

By the evening of the 6th March everything was again ready for the road, and on the following morning at daybreak a start was made. The long *cortége* had hardly set out when a loud roaring was heard, and Lieutenant Valliere exclaimed, " A lion ! It cannot be far off. Is it a good omen, or not ? "

" It comes from the *right*," replied Dr. Tautain jestingly.

" However it be," said Captain Gallieni, " Forward's the word."

The first halt was made at the village of Golmi, the forest of Goura having been crossed during the march, which lay along the left bank of the Senegal. Everything was ready for a bivouac, and the ass-drivers began to prepare their rice and couscous, under the direction of the *chef de cuisine* Yoro. Yoro was an important personage in the expedition, and merits more than a passing mention.

He was a Toucouleur of the Laobé tribe; a people held in slight esteem by their countrymen, by reason of their gaining their livelihood by cutting wood, digging ditches, and making pestles for crushing the meal for couscous. In many parts of Africa the greatest disdain is manifested for the working castes, such as weavers, rope-makers, and smiths. The Laobés, who are spread throughout all Senegal, live apart, and marry among themselves, but are nevertheless one of the most prosperous tribes in the country.

Yoro was of a type frequently met with among the native races who have taken on a varnish of civilization. He was vain, a liar, and a thief; but he had also good qualities. He was a capital fellow in a crisis. He got the breakfast ready with a marvellous expedition, and could prepare for dinner the most tempting dishes. He had been in turn tirailleur, scullion, muleteer, sailor; always greedy, always miserable, and always absolutely devoted to his master. When evil fortune befell, Yoro would sell his dearest possession in order to satisfy our desires. More than once he proved his devotion to Captain Gallieni by exposing his body to the bullets of hostile natives in defence of his master. At Nango, where Gallieni was struck down with fever, Yoro sat day and night by the sick man's bed, and nursed him with the gentleness of a mother. It is no wonder, therefore, that Captain Gallieni speaks of his faithful attendant in terms of affectionate esteem.

The expedition left Golmi on the 8th, and arrived next at Guoy, a province of Bakel. Here long chains of hills stretch towards the south; but on the other side of the river the country is flat, and the *marigots* are the only obstacles which interrupted the march. By marigots is meant those small affluents of the Senegal which, dry as a rule for the most part of the year, overflow in the rainy season and form deep and wide channels. After crossing the river Falémé, a beautiful stream which discharges a considerable volume of water into the Senegal, the expedition entered Kaméra. The inhabitants of Kaméra are a peaceable and hard-working people, who bear the cognomen of the "Jews of Soudan." Kaméra is under the protectorate of France. The surrounding country presents no features of special interest—forest and brushwood, varied here and there by a small stream, and in the vicinity of the villages fields planted with millet.

On the morning of March 11th, the camp was pitched before the village of Goré, an important centre inhabited by Bambarras, who escaped the sword of Amadou on the occasion of his last raid upon Kaarta in 1874. Dama, the chief of Goré, gave the travellers a very hearty reception, presenting Gallieni with beef, mutton, milk, etc.; and to do special honour to his guests, he arranged for their diversion a *tom-tom*, or military *fête*.

Gallieni and his comrades were conducted with much ceremony by the king's chief ministers to the scene of action—a band of musicians leading the way, and making on their rude instruments the most indescribable uproar. Dama himself was seated, cross-legged, on a leopard's skin stretched on the ground. About him were grouped his warriors in various attitudes, armed with guns and lances.

The night was dark, and the vast crowd, itself as black as the night, and lit up only by sundry torches, presented a strange and most fantastic appearance. Captain Gallieni was seated beside the king, and presently the dance began. It was engaged in by men only, and these the most nobly born and the bravest in the state. The *tom-toms*, a kind of long drums, which give the name to the ceremony; trumpets of hollow wood, uttering a harsh and monotonous sound; and little flutes, played in a rather melodious fashion—these formed the orchestra. The trumpets emitted three notes only, always the same, and all sad and mournful, producing a most melancholy effect upon the ear.

While the music was at its height, the dancers arranged themselves in many various attitudes in the flaring light of the torches, each warrior grasping his gun or sabre. Now they stooped, now tossed their weapons in the air, now pirouetted, and now threw their arms above their heads; always dancing in time, their eyes flashing with a warlike fire. The dancers won the enthusiastic applause of the spectators, and the *fête* terminated with a display of coloured lights which Captain Gallieni caused to be burned for the wonder and delight of the simple natives.

On the 12th March, the explorers camped on the bank of the river at the village of Ambidédi, under the shadow of three noble bread-fruit trees, whose trunks measured between fifteen and twenty yards in circumference, and whose leafy boughs made an impervious screen against the sun. Towards evening shots were heard on the right bank. It was one of those affrays which are continually taking place between the Moors and the Sarracolets of Guidimakha, the origin of which is always the same—the wish on the part of the Moors to possess themselves of their neighbours' herds, and the determination of the rightful owners to defend their property.

After traversing a very fertile region, planted with beautiful fields of millet, the village of Bongourou was reached on the 14th, and shortly after Mediné, which is two hundred and sixty leagues from the mouth of the Senegal, and situated near the cataract of Félou. Here Captain Gallieni halted for some days, to reorganize and strengthen the expedition.

At this time, it being the dry season, the country around Mediné was dry and parched and almost destitute of pasturage. The camp was pitched to the south of the village, under the shadow of two or three lofty trees, on a plain encircled by rocky hills. The Senegal was not far off, the main river alone being able to supply sufficient water for the wants of the expedition. All the smaller streams were dry.

The site of the camp was remarkable in several respects. A semicircle of lofty rocks, absolutely vertical, formed the background. The face of the rock was broken by frequent cavities, the haunt of innumerable monkeys, and of hyenas that come down at night into the very streets of Mediné and utter their hoarse cries under the walls of the fort.

From the camp could be seen also the "Lion Rocks;" so called from their peculiar formation— huge masses of rock resembling crouching lions.

By this time the expedition, which had been strengthened from stage to stage during the journey, presented a really imposing array. The camp was divided into sections, each under the command of its own leader, each bearing conspicuous its own flag. Thus far the most perfect order had been preserved in every department; and never before, probably, had the natives beheld so numerous and well-equipped a caravan.

From Mediné to Bafoulabé the valley of the Senegal rises gradually from an elevation of about thirty to nearly one hundred yards. Beyond Boukaria, transport by water is no longer practicable—the course of the river being here broken by numerous small falls and rapids, not to mention the cataract of Gouina.

While Gallieni remained at Mediné, the first difficulty which he had experienced with his followers arose. The Toucouleurs, with characteristic fickleness, had lost the enthusiasm for the journey which they had at first shown, and began to think they were not sufficiently remunerated for their labours. The seeds of a conspiracy were being sown, and the malcontents, urged on by two or three leaders, threatened to abandon the white man unless more favourable terms were granted them. Captain Gallieni's action in this crisis was sufficiently prompt and energetic to quell at once the threatened outbreak. Nevertheless, he could not but feel some slight uneasiness at the idea of being deserted by his native escort—a danger which so frequently menaces the African explorer, and which, by causing delay and other mortifications, so imperils the success of an expedition.

By the 21st March the travellers were again ready for the journey. Such of the asses as had been disabled during the march from Bakel to Mediné were replaced by others; fresh native horses had been purchased, as well as a herd of cattle to provide fresh meat for the expedition. The chiefs of Mediné gave a dinner in honour of Captain Gallieni and his comrades on the eve of their departure. Finally, on the morning of the start the explorers were treated to a serenade by the chief musician of Mediné. The performance was sufficiently diverting, for it consisted of a medley of native and French airs, the latter selected from the operas of "La Grande Duchesse" and "La Fille de Madame Angot." The effect of the lively French music sung by the swarthy troubadour to the accompaniment of his rude guitar was singular and amusing.

The first difficulty which the caravan had to encounter occurred almost at the gates of Mediné. The valley of the Senegal, enclosed at this point between two walls of cliffs, is completely barred by a mass of rocks known as the plateau of Félou, behind which stretches the beautiful plain of Logo. Here there are the genuine traces of a dike which once held a portion of the waters of the Senegal, and formed a large lagoon, having for its bed the plain of Logo. On the Mediné side the plateau terminates suddenly and abruptly in rocky pinnacles.

The Senegal has broken down this dike on the right side, and has channelled for itself a straight course towards the steep cliffs; but a line of rocks still bars the progress of the river, and, by holding the waters within the plain of Logo, forms a magnificent sheet of water stretching as far as Boukaria. That barrier, hollowed, worn, polished, sculptured in a fashion, by the friction of the waters, presents a most picturesque appearance—vaults from which the water drips drop by drop, cascades, caverns with inaccessible recesses, caldrons shaped like upturned cones by pebbles of adamantine hardness, which are kept in continual circular motion by separate currents.

The plateau of Félou did not prove so great an obstacle to progress as Captain Gallieni, from previous knowledge of the locality, had anticipated. For it was now the dry season, and by following the empty water-courses channelled in the plains, it was not very difficult to reach the slope leading to the plain of Logo.

On the morning of the 22nd the village of Sabouciré was reached, the scene of a brilliant foray made by Colonel Reybaud against the Malinkés of Logo, who had rebelled against the authority of Sambala, an old ally of the French.

After halting at several intermediate stations, including Malou and Dinguira—the latter a beautiful village, well built and well cultivated—the travellers reached the famous cataract of Gouina, the crash of whose waters was heard long before the fall itself was in sight. In the winter season the Gouina cataract discharges into the great basin below an immense volume of water; and the current is so strong that hippopotami are often swept over the fall from the upper waters and found crushed among the rocks below. In the dry season the appearance of the cataract is less imposing but more graceful. The rocks, rising above the current, present a smooth and polished surface; and the water gleams and glistens among the crevasses like strings of iridescent pearls, falling in little cascades on the successive terraces of rock in a way that entrances the gaze.

The camp was pitched over against Foukhara, a little village built on an island in the middle of the stream—a somewhat inconvenient position by reason of the innumerable hippopotami which infest the Senegal, and which have to be frightened off by the nightly beating of drums.

Two days were occupied in the journey from Foukhara to the Talahari—the route followed leading through a veritable desert. At this stage the leader was attacked with violent fever; but, thanks to the prompt and efficacious treatment of Dr. Bayol, he was soon able to accomplish the last stage of the journey to Bafoulabé. The village of Makhina was passed, and the left bank of the Bafing reached.

Bafoulabé stands at the confluence of the two streams which form the Senegal—a name which signifies "two rivers." The more important of these is the Bafing, or Black River. It flows from the south, and has its source in the mountain masses of Fouta

Djalon. The other confluent is the Bakhoy, or White River, flowing from the east.

Bafoulabé had been chosen as the site of the first of those stations which the French desired to establish as far as the Joliba, the great river of the negroes. On the morning of the 2nd April, Captain Gallieni had the satisfaction of beholding all his forces, men and animals, drawn up in good order on the little plateau which was to serve as the site of the new station of Bafoulabé.

Captain Gallieni had now entered a country in which the faculty of the diplomatist was as essential as that of the explorer. His directions were, that he should follow the valley of the Bakhoy, which is the shortest route to the Niger. Time pressed, and it was expedient to reach the Joliba before winter. Accordingly, the order was given to leave Bafoulabé on 2nd April.

The march led through forest country thickly planted with lofty and beautiful trees. Some of these were of singular shape and appearance. Their trunks, curiously indented at the base, formed, as it were, niches, with regularly-shaped walls, which became gradually merged in the tree itself at a distance of four or five yards above the ground. One of these giants of the forest measured nearly twenty yards in circumference.

Birds of varied and brilliant plumage fluttered

among the leafy boughs overhead, making a lively and pleasant music. Among the most conspicuous of these was a bird resembling an English pheasant, its head adorned with a pretty black crest, its plumage a beautiful dark blue.

The left bank of the Bakhoy was followed as closely as possible; but the luxuriant vegetation prevented any careful examination of its course. Night fell before the camp was pitched, which occasioned some disorder. But a circumstance which served still further to increase the confusion, and to place the caravan in actual danger for a few moments, was a fire which broke out a little way from the camp almost before the different sections were fairly settled. It was the dry season, which the natives utilize in clearing their fallow fields of parasitic vegetation. It was not a little startling to see the flames rushing heavenwards so close to the camp, reddening the sky and horizon. The high grass blazed with marvellous rapidity, crackling and roaring with a noise that could be heard miles away. The gigantic baobab trees, with their branches resembling human arms, seemed to tremble with terror, and presented a most fantastic appearance in the wavering glare of the flames.

The wind was blowing towards the camp, and not a minute was to be lost if the threatened danger was to be avoided. Already some of the asses, terrified

FIRE ON THE LEFT BANK OF THE BAKHOY, NEAR DEMBA-DIOUBE.

Page 178.

by the noise, had thrown off their loads and broken loose into the forest. A number of the men, providing themselves with large and leafy branches, advanced towards the fire. Leaping, shouting, dancing, gesticulating, like true negroes as they were, they had soon mastered the flames, at least over a sufficient area to preclude all immediate danger to the camp.

On the following day the explorers reached the village of Kala, after skirting the mountain of Douka and crossing a number of dry tributaries of the main river. The river Bakhoy, from Bafoulabé as far as its confluence with the Baoulé, flows through a wide valley sloping from east to west and flanked on each side by mountain masses.

On the 4th the village of Niakalé Ciréa was reached, and the camp pitched beneath a beautiful fig-tree. Here a somewhat disagreeable incident befell Captain Gallieni. The young chief, Gara Mamady Ciré, whom the leader had commanded to follow him to the Niger, arrived on the 5th with a large following of armed men, contrary to Captain Gallieni's injunctions. The chief began first to complain that to him, the son of a great chief, had been given a less beautiful horse than Alpha Sega, the interpreter, had received. Then he declared that he could not follow Captain Gallieni unless he were allowed to take with him forty men of his village. Captain Gallieni understood perfectly that this untractable warrior had no great desire to trust himself in an unknown country, dangerous to traverse by reason of the continual warfare which prevailed. He told the chief in plain and vigorous terms that he might take himself off home again as soon as he pleased; to which Gara replied with equanimity, assuring the white man that he was depriving himself of an important ally in leaving him, Gara, behind.

Gallieni and his lieutenants had scarcely forgotten the disagreeable feeling produced by this incident, when an episode of a more amusing character occurred. A sheep had just been purchased from a Malinké; and Yoro the cook had already begun to cut up and prepare the animal for dinner, when the late proprietor returned, rending the air with the most piteous cries, and regretting in the bitterest terms the bargain he had just concluded. He bewailed and gesticulated, exclaiming, "Is it possible that I could have allowed myself to be so taken in? What! one little piece for an animal which lives, which walks, which eats, which drinks! Is it right—is it just?" It is impossible, Captain Gallieni writes, to convey the manner and the complaints, each more ludicrous than the other, of the aggrieved Malinké; the simple truth being, that he wished, over and above his price, a calabash of brandy, which he at last got.

After quitting Niakalé Ciréa, the march became difficult and painful, leading through a long gorge

VILLAGE OF SOLINTA, ON THE BAKHOY.

where the ground was broken and rugged with huge blocks of rock. The camp was next pitched at the village of Solinta, by the ford of the Dioubé Ba.

The sun had hardly set when the hyenas began to prowl around the camp with their hoarse and melancholy howling, their lean flanks and hideous forms revealed strangely in the light of the camp-fires. They approached quite close, attracted by the *débris* of the supper. A discharge of shot was not sufficient to frighten off these frequent and objectionable guests of every African bivouac.

Presently, too, a disturbance among the asses, followed by a loud roaring, warned the travellers of the presence of another night foe—namely, lions. The shots had, however, apparently frightened these last visitors, and their roaring ere long ceased. The lions of Senegambia are maneless. They rarely attack men; but it was seldom that our travellers pitched their camp without the roaring of these kings of the forest coming to disturb their slumbers. One of the sharp-shooters, however, was on one occasion attacked by a lion, and only escaped by climbing a large tree, the thick branches and dense foliage of which served him for a refuge for the night.

At the village of Solinta, where the caravan halted, the attention of Captain Gallieni and his comrades was arrested by a large furnace of remarkable construction. It was built in the earth, almost cylindrical in shape, and widening towards the centre. This furnace was employed in the manufacture of iron for making swords, knives, and other utensils used by the natives of the region.

The neighbouring mountains supply the minerals for the furnace in great abundance. Many workmen are employed in working it. It is furnished with a number of mouths, to which are fitted bellows worked by hand. One other mouth, much larger than the rest, is kept open when the operation of smelting the metal is about to begin. When a sufficient quantity of metal is ready for smelting, all the smiths of the village give themselves to the work at the same time. The occasion becomes in some sort a festival as well as a labour, for the workmen are plied with copious draughts of maize-beer. Songs and shrill cries accompany the work, the roaring of the fires swells the din, and every man bears a hand at the bellows until the metal is ready. Captain Gallieni remarks that a very similar method of iron-forging obtains in the Pyrenees.

The 8th of the month was spent by the expedition at Soukoutaly, the chief of which, a fine old man of frank and resolute bearing, evinced much satisfaction when Captain Gallieni explained to him his projects in regard to the Upper Niger. The old chief was greatly pleased when the white leader said that he had often heard of him, and presented him, on behalf of M. Brière de l'Isle, with a handsome mantle and a gun mounted with silver.

At Soukoutaly Captain Gallieni received further proof of the hatred in which the Toucouleurs are held in these regions. The chief men of Tomora, a country subject to the king of Segou, sought Gallieni, asking if they and all their people might be allowed to cross the river and take up their abode within the protection of the new station of Bafoulabé. Captain Gallieni answered, that it was not part of his scheme to mix himself up with the affairs of Amadou, but that his petitioners could do as they pleased. The men understood what was meant, and Captain Gallieni afterwards learned that they had put their project into execution.

The empire of Amadou is now but the relic of the vast conquests of the prophet El Hadj Oumar, and is fast losing power and prestige. The peoples of Malinké and Bambarra have long groaned under its intolerable yoke, and only wait an opportunity of breaking free from the domination of the Mussulman, the worst enemy of both the white and black races in this part of Africa.

Journeying across a fertile region, the explorers presently arrived at Badumbé. Badumbé is surrounded by a wall of solid masonry—one of the most remarkable constructions met with by the travellers in Africa. The object of this embattlement was no doubt to protect the inhabitants against the attacks of the Toucouleurs. In shape it approached a quadrilateral, and was naturally protected on one side by the Bakhoy, on two other sides by affluents of that river, and on the fourth by the mountains. The enclosure was a polygon, containing a round tower furnished with a sally-port. The wall of the tower followed a zigzag course, which enabled those holding the fort to open a cross fire as well as a direct fire. Lofty parapets allowed also of a fire being kept up from without.

The people of Badumbé received the expedition with much cordiality, regarding them as the enemies of the Toucouleurs. One brought a sheep, another a chicken, a third a calabash of milk, a fourth a bag of corn for Captain Gallieni's horse—all vied in showing attention to the strangers.

At Badumbé the caravan remained one day, encamped on a hot and desolate plain, under the very inadequate shade of two or three acacia trees. The white men were an object of much curiosity to the natives of the place; their clothes, and especially their trowsers, exciting much wonder and amusement. One of the young negresses asked to be allowed to touch Captain Gallieni's bare arm, that she might assure herself that the flesh was the same as her own.

The nearer the explorers approached to the Niger, the difficulties of the journey increased. The further they advanced, the slighter their knowledge grew of the ground they were traversing, and the less prepared were they to meet the obstacles of the march.

Beyond Badumbé the valley widens considerably and becomes more undulating. The Bakhoy describes towards the north the arc of a circle, and the path leading to Fangalla follows the circumference of that arc.

An elephant-hunter of Badumbé was found to act as guide to the expedition as far as Fangalla. The route led through a forest where it was often necessary to cut a path for the animals with the sword.

Fangalla was once the capital of Farimboula, and its populous villages stretched along the banks of the Bakhoy and over the islands which dot its waters. The king of Fangalla was rich in herds and flocks, and the people were prosperous and brave. But thirty years ago a horde of Mussulmans swept down on Fangalla, plundered its inhabitants, harried their cattle, devastated the fields, and retired, leaving behind them desolation and ruin. It may be said, generally, that wherever the followers of the Prophet pass in Africa, misery and ruin follow in their wake.

On the morning of the 13th the caravan reached the falls of Bily. At this point in its course, the river, confined between two rocky cliffs, falls in successive cascades to form the cataract, which is of considerable height and volume, and resembles the Gouina fall. The water falls vertically; the rocks are smooth and polished, and, worn in many places by the current and the pebbles, form little subterranean streams which unite their several waters with the main cataract as it tumbles with a crash into the basin below.

Beyond the Bily fall the path pursued by the travellers led again along the river, and was with difficulty followed, owing to the stony character of the ground. The country, bare in certain parts, was covered in others with absolutely virgin forest;—acacias of very graceful shape; tamarinds of dense and beautiful foliage; *khadd* trees, whose falling leaves foretold the approach of winter; and fig-trees, on which parasitic roots drooped to the ground from the higher branches like the cordage of a ship. The whole forest was densely interlaced with creeping plants which hung their festoons from tree to tree, and proved a formidable obstacle to the progress of the caravan, obliging the constant use of hatchet and sword. The horsemen were ever and anon compelled to bend low to avoid the branches and threatening thorns. The mules, becoming frequently entangled among the boughs, found the march a most difficult one; but as the good-natured old Sambo, one of Captain Gallieni's native companions, said, laughing his great laugh, while the leader was watching the baggage with an anxious eye, "Fear nothing, captain; believe me, the cargo is solid."

FOREST NEAR THE BILY FALLS, ON THE BAKHOY.

Page 190.

On the 14th the passage of the Bakhoy began. The first section of the caravan led the way; all the ass-drivers, carrying their baggage on their heads, entered the stream, taking care not to fall on the slippery rocks of the ford. The baggage having been got safely across, the asses had to be led over. Then followed the muleteers and spahis, each leading his beast by the bridle and carrying his saddle on his head. Lastly came Captain Gallieni, with naked feet and legs, feeling his way with a stick.

By mid-day the crossing was successfully accomplished, and the whole camp was treated, in honour of the event, to a double ration of meat and rice. Across this broad river there had been transported, in the course of a few hours, six hundred and fifty loads of baggage and nearly four hundred horses, mules, oxen, and asses.

During the afternoon Captain Gallieni took the opportunity of the halt to send for three of the ass-drivers who had frequently of late signalized themselves by their laziness and insubordination. The caravan was in the middle of the desert, and the poor wretches cast themselves at Captain Gallieni's feet and implored pardon, declaring that for the future they would be models of obedience. Two of them were willing to resume their duties as ass-drivers; but the third, Mamadou Si, a turbulent and surly Toucouleur, refused. This man had already shown at Bakel his insubordinate spirit, and at Mediné had instigated a conspiracy that had all but deprived Captain Gallieni of twenty of his followers. On that occasion the leader restrained himself from doing as he would have liked; but at Toukoto he seized the opportunity of a complaint which Mamadou Si made against the chief of his section, to expel the unruly member from the camp—a severe but deserved and necessary punishment.

The sojourn of the explorers at Goniokori was fraught with special interest, as will be presently seen. Goniokori is composed of three separate villages built at intervals of three or four hundred yards, in a plain of great fertility and planted with beautiful breadfruit and cedar trees. The grand mountain mass of Badougou lies to the north, the peak of Gotékrou to the east, a rocky plateau extends to the south, while the Bakhoy bounds the plain on the west. The three villages together do not contain more than five hundred inhabitants, but represent, nevertheless, the capital of Fouladougou, that extensive territory which embraces all the country between Kaarta-Bélédougou, and Manding.

Captain Gallieni was much surprised at the poverty and barbarity of the king and people of Goniokori. He had expected to find a rich and powerful chief, for he was the descendant of an ancient line of kings. The reception which he gave to the leaders of the expedi-

THE REFRACTORY ASS-DRIVERS.
Page 103.

tion was a mixture of indifference and awe. Its great numbers evidently caused him more fear than joy; and although Captain Gallieni endeavoured to make it clear to him that the white men had come to assist him against his foes the Toucouleurs, the chief did not seem to comprehend, and his attitude remained one of mingled resignation and imbecility.

This singular chief had a brother who governed one of the three villages. This brother was as noisy and demonstrative as the other was reserved and indifferent. From the excitement of his speech and gestures it was easily seen that this fellow was drunk. An old negress, also manifestly the worse for *dolo*,* followed him like his shadow, speaking in a thick and inarticulate fashion, graced with many hiccoughs.

Finding that he could make nothing of the royal drunkard, Captain Gallieni addressed himself to an old man who had been regarding the white men with an air of much interest, and who now pushed his way through the crowd of women and children whom curiosity had collected around the strangers.

This old man informed Captain Gallieni and his companions that on the spot where the camp was now pitched had stood the house of Mansa Numma, the king of all Fouladougou, then a rich and powerful monarch. "One day—I was not born then," continued the man—"a man of strange appearance

---

* An intoxicating drink made of fermented millet.

appeared on the left bank of the river, in front of the village. He called out in an unknown language, and, seeing that no one understood his words, plunged into the river and landed in the midst of the chief men who were gathered on the bank. One gave him a house for the night, another brought couscous and milk, and all treated him hospitably. In departing, the white chief left behind him fine presents. He showed himself kind and generous, and amply repaid the king for his hospitality by presenting him with a beautiful silver bracelet. That bracelet had always been worn by the head of the royal family, until the fatal day when El Hadj pillaged the treasure of the chiefs of Fouladougou, and carried away the bracelet to Ségou." The speaker concluded by saying that the white men whom he was addressing were richer than the one who had come long ago, and that they would show themselves equally generous by replacing the lost bracelet, and by making other presents still more beautiful.

This speech was listened to by Captain Gallieni and his companions with the greatest interest. It was the first traces they had come upon of Mungo Park, their predecessor in these regions, and the explorers experienced a legitimate satisfaction in resting on the spot which the illustrious English traveller had chosen for his encampment sixty-five years ago, and where no European had been since. Captain

Gallieni, having consulted the narrative of that pioneer of African exploration, discovered a trifling detail omitted by the old Malinké—namely, that the white man had been robbed by the grandfather of the then reigning king.

The next halt was made at Manambougou, a little village enclosed between the peak of Gotékrou and a lofty mountain range, and lying at the bottom of a lovely valley. The fortunate inhabitants of this beautiful little corner of the world are very different in character from their savage neighbours of Goniokori, being docile, quiet, and remarkably well clothed. The chief, accompanied by several of his suite, came to welcome the white men, with much natural dignity—a noble old man, with a tranquil and intelligent face, wearing a long and very becoming cloak, a turban on his head, and bearing a fine carved staff in his hand. His costume and bearing recalled in no slight degree the figures of the Bible patriarchs. Captain Gallieni learned that the old chief had travelled a great deal, and that he was well beloved by his people.

Beyond Manambougou the march became very difficult. It led up a rocky incline, debouching on a plateau sloping towards the east, and covered with ferruginous gray-stone, slippery for the feet, and offering a very toilsome path for the animals.

At length the Kégnéko was gained. This small

stream is from fifteen to twenty yards broad, and about fifteen feet in depth. The men, under the direction of Sergeant Sadioka and Corporal Bénis, began to construct an impromptu bridge across the river. Two large trees were felled, one on each side of the stream, and their trunks, falling crosswise, formed a sort of letter X. Along the arms of the letter branches were laid longitudinally, and on these again were spread leafy shoots of the bamboo, together with ferns and grass. When the whole was covered with turf, a bridge was formed sufficiently strong and secure, across which the whole caravan passed in safety.

A long and difficult march brought the travellers to Bondoro, a village in the Kita country, and they were presently at the base of the famous mountain of Kita. An hour later, the young King Tokonta met the strangers at the entrance of his village, and bade them welcome with great courtesy.

Tokonta had got ready for the accommodation of his guests a spacious hut, which, however, was found to be too near the village. The camp was accordingly pitched at a distance of three or four hundred yards off, in the middle of the plain. The first goal of the expedition had now been reached, and the leader judged it expedient to rest his followers and himself for a few days, before taking the route for the Niger.

Kita—or rather Makadiambougo, for Kita is the

IMPROVISED BRIDGE OVER THE KEGNEKO.

name of the whole region—may be called the key of all this part of the Soudan, and in a commercial aspect occupies a position of the greatest importance. On one side it commands the road to the Niger, and on the other that leading to the territories of the Moors.

The object of the expedition at Kita was to conclude a treaty with the king, which should place the country under the protectorate of France. Captain Gallieni hoped to establish at Makadiambougo a military and commercial station, which might open up a way to central Soudan. He began, therefore, without delay negotiations with Tokonta. But he was met at the outset with difficulties, unexpected but easy enough of explanation.

Kita is very near Mourgoula, the Toucouleur fortress which holds in subjection all the Malinké population, from Manding as far as Fouladougou. On the other hand, Nioro, ruled by Mountaga, the brother of the king of Ségou, is not far off towards the north. Thus the king of Kita finds himself most inconveniently situated between two enemies, and has often, to avoid ruin to himself, to separate his cause from that of the other Malinké peoples, and to take no part in their attempts at revolt. He must take every occasion of proving his fidelity to Amadou. It is easily understood, therefore, why Tokonta hesitated about allying himself to the French, the declared enemies of the Toucouleurs. "No doubt," said he, "the

French are rich and powerful; but they are far away from my country."

Days passed in these negotiations. Tokonta maintained a silent and reserved attitude, though, in truth, he was in great agitation as to the outcome of the parley. Alpha Sega, the interpreter to the expedition, received *carte-blanche* in regard to presents with which to win over the chief. The interviews between Alpha Sega and the native notables were accompanied by a large consumption of dolo, or maize beer, of which all the Malinké nations are extremely fond; and often did the interpreter return at night to Captain Gallieni, to report the result of the day's parley, with his utterance much impaired by the severe labours of the day.

At length Captain Gallieni and his lieutenants hit upon a device to bring the wavering Tokonta to a final decision. The chief was at feud with the neighbouring village of Goubanko, and the French leader threatened, unless the king came to terms, to treat with the enemy. An envoy was actually despatched to Goubanko to carry out this project. Tokonta became alarmed, and, after a little further parley, agreed to sign the treaty.

On the 25th April, the king of Kita, surrounded by his sons and the chiefs and notables, set his signature to the document which placed all the Kita territory under the protectorate of France, and authorized that nation to erect, on any site they might choose, such stations and establishments as they should judge fit.

Captain Gallieni desired to celebrate this signal episode in the history of the mission in some fitting way, and at the desire of Tokonta a military spectacle was arranged by the expedition.

All the preliminaries being ready, the camp presented a quite brilliant appearance. The tirailleurs and the spahis, wearing their handsome Oriental costumes, formed one side of a square. The muleteers and ass-drivers had also exchanged their travel-worn clothes of every day for bright white and blue jackets, which were kept stowed away for grand occasions such as the present. The black sailors did duty as artillerymen, taking up their position at one angle of the square. The leaders themselves had donned handsome cloaks of white flannel, slashed with black; and in a word, everything was done to excite the imagination of the Malinkés, who crowded from every quarter to be present at the spectacle. As for Alpha Sega, the interpreter, he shone resplendent in a grand Turkish military costume, covered with gold braiding—a dress which was destined for Amadou, but which was lent to Alpha Sega for this occasion. In the centre of the square a tall flagstaff was raised, from which fluttered a large tricolor: and Captain Gallieni records how the hearts of himself and his companions beat at beholding their national colours floating over the plains of Kita, the possession of which secured to France all the valley of the Bakhoy, the direct route to the Niger.

The tirailleurs executed their various military movements; then the rapid discharge of the chassepots excited the wonder of the savage spectators. But the enthusiasm rose to a height when the spahis, wearing their turbans and beautiful red mantles, curveted over the plain, cutting the air this way and that with their sabres, their handsome horses at full gallop. During these manœuvres the ass-drivers fired their guns, and the small cannons manned by the black sailors kept up an unceasing fusilade. Never before had the onlookers beheld a scene so striking, and their admiration approached stupefaction.

Thus the negotiations at Kita were terminated with *éclat*, and lengthy despatches were sent off to M. Briere de l'Isle, under the care of a son of Tokonta, advising him of the success of the mission thus far.

The departure of the expedition from Kita took place on April 27th. The beasts of burden had suffered much of late from sore backs, and several of the mules and asses were dying every day. Twenty-one animals died in all, and their loads had to be distributed among the surviving mules and asses, already reduced almost to the extremity of weakness. Fortunately, a rich plain was presently reached, which

REVIEW ON THE PLAINS OF KITA TO CELEBRATE THE TREATY OF PROTECTORATE WITH FRANCE.

afforded an ample supply of grass; and soon after, the caravan halted on the banks of the Bandingho.

Dr. Tautain immediately set about devising measures for crossing the river. The passage looked impracticable. Steep banks, between thirty and forty feet high, formed a lofty barrier, blocked up with great masses of gray stone. The right bank, rising in a peak, was composed of stiff red clay, almost as hard as rock. The left bank was a little less difficult of access, and led to a ford not very deep, and sufficiently easy to cross.

Dr. Tautain applied himself to the situation with zeal. The tirailleurs succeeded in making a sort of staircase for the animals in the left bank; but shovel and pick were of little avail against the stiff soil of the opposite bank, and the workmen had to be content with constructing a rough and irregular escalade.

The mules had now to be got across this stairway. The muleteers, assisted by the spahis and tirailleurs, endeavoured to make the crossing; but it was labour lost. They easily enough descended the pathway made in the left bank, but were altogether unable to ascend the cliff on the right bank. At this juncture Sambo came to the rescue. Disengaging one of the long cords that secured the loads, he passed it round the croup of a mule, while the two ends were grasped by men standing on the top of the bank. A muleteer, grasping hold of some bushes which had contrived to take root in that hard soil, dragged the mule by the bridle. At a given signal, the poor beast, dragged by the bridle and pulled by the rope from above, was at last hoisted to the top of the cliff.

About mid-day the ford presented a curious scene;—one of the cliffs covered with animals with long-eared heads, all pointed towards the river; the other bank crowded with the tirailleurs still engaged in finishing the escalade, and hard at work with pick and shovel; mid-way an odd medley of asses thirstily drinking, natives assisting in getting the animals across, and doing all with faces of almost preternatural gravity,—the whole picture framed in by the great trees which covered the lofty banks of the Bandingho.

At last, an hour after sunset, the work was over and the transit of the entire caravan completed. No mishap had befallen, and the fatigues of the day were quickly forgotten by all over a good dinner.

The march was resumed on the following day in good order and in good spirits. On the 30th April the caravan passed the mountains of Bangassi, the sight of which recalled to the travellers recollections of Mungo Park, who makes mention of this range in his journal. The surrounding country is desolate and barren.

The caravan at this stage began to suffer from thirst, and Alassane and two others of the guides were sent forward to search for water. Fortunately an

CROSSING THE BANDINGHO. *Page 209.*

abundant water-course was discovered not far off, and on its banks the camp was pitched. The borders of the stream were covered with the tracks of animals of large size, among which were the prints of lions, antelopes, and giraffes.

Rain fell in deluges during the night, and the camp was well-nigh inundated. Little sleep was enjoyed by any one, and the day was welcomed with relief. This heavy rainfall warned the travellers of the approach of winter—an uneasy thought, for the flooding of the rivers and creeks would considerably increase the difficulties of the march, while the damp malarious weather would, in all probability, materially lower the general health of the camp.

Gallieni had ever present in his memory that ill-fated expedition of Mungo Park in this very region, when his comrades perished one by one. Out of thirty-nine who accompanied that explorer from Gambia, five alone returned with him to Bammakoo.

The morning of May 1st was entirely occupied in "drying the camp"—tents, blankets, saddles, and raiment—a mighty fire having been built for this purpose. Suddenly, while engaged in this business, the general attention was attracted by a loud noise and movement in that part of the camp nearest the river. Everybody—spahis, tirailleurs, muleteers, and ass-drivers—rushed to the bank, brandishing all kinds of weapons,—guns, swords, lances, sticks; Yoro the *chef* among the rest, interrupted while in the preparation of dinner, flourishing his cook's knife. Old Sambo declared that the cause of the commotion was a tiger, which, surprised by a spahi who had been taking his horse to drink, had plunged into the river.

Captain Gallieni and the other leaders seized their rifles, and were immediately in the thick of the crowd. N'Gor Faye, the hunter of Kobaboulinda, was already mid-way in the stream in pursuit of the creature which had raised such a commotion. The throng on the bank shouted and gesticulated, making an uproar of which it was impossible to discover the real cause. For a long time the object of the chase remained beneath the water in a manner that made it difficult to believe the creature either a tiger or a panther. At length there appeared above the surface the head of a large otter, which soon fell the prey of N'Gor Faye. When Sambo was rallied about his tiger, he was equal to the occasion, replying, "Well, the otter is the water-tiger!"

The next most important halt made by the expedition was at Koundou, the principal village of Fouladougou, containing some seven or eight hundred inhabitants. Lieutenant Valliere, in advance of the main body of the caravan, had prepared the way for the reception of the expedition at Koundou. He had been met by the chief and his warriors in a hilarious and excited condition from over-draughts of dolo.

But on the following day, when the effects of the revel had disappeared, the king and notables of Koundou had listened favourably to Lieutenant Valliere's overtures, accompanied as they were by a present of cloths. Thus when Captain Gallieni arrived with the main body he was hospitably welcomed by the Koundou chieftain.

The river Baoulé divides the Malinkés from the Bambarras, the Fouladougou country from the Bélédougou. The latter is a fine country, well watered by the Baoulé and its affluents, and characterized by the luxuriance of its vegetation. Some two hundred and fifty villages, hidden in dells and hollows, and surrounded with strong walls, occupy the cleared spaces in the forest. The inhabitants of this vast territory are at constant feud among themselves or with their neighbours, and live almost entirely by pillage.

The Fouladougou natives showed a hostile front to the expedition. At Guinina, when Captain Gallieni sought an interview with the chief, a handsome old man of stalwart carriage, the latter received the white leader coldly, and told him plainly that he neither trusted him nor understood his intentions.

"For whom," said he, "are all these presents that you bring with you?"

The unfriendliness of the negro king was evident, and Captain Gallieni felt sure that he would lose no favourable opportunity of showing it. Under these circumstances the leader took all expedient precautions against possible surprise. The camp was strengthened and protected as far as it could be by piling up the baggage so as to form a sort of rampart. The spahis and muleteers were stationed on guard on one side of the encampment, the tirailleurs on the other, while the animals were placed in the middle, where also the tent of the leaders was pitched. At the angles of the square thus formed were placed the guns (mounted on carriages constructed from the trunks of trees), directed upon the gates of the village, and on the forest surrounding the open space where the camp was pitched.

In the evening the guard of spahis and tirailleurs was doubled, and from time to time Captain Gallieni caused coloured lights and rockets to be discharged, with the object of striking awe into the hearts of the natives. Later in the night, when all was silent about the camp, a patrol of the village walls was made, when a loud noise as of men in eager discussion was heard within. Two of Captain Gallieni's native followers who understood the Bambarra language announced that the debate referred to an attack upon the white men, who "had come into the Bélédougou country to deceive the people, and to aid the Toucouleurs in subjugating them."

On the following morning, May 9th, Captain Gallieni sent to ask the Guinina chief for guides for the journey, when the old king, who had shown himself so cold on the previous day, not only proposed to send guides but also men to help in carrying the baggage. Captain Gallieni, however, was not duped by this excess of complaisance. Next day, the old man, impressed no doubt by seeing the guns directed upon the walls of his village, did actually provide five guides chosen from his own household, in return for which service he was to receive a satisfactory present —four pieces of yellow cloth, six swords, a keg of rum, etc. Captain Gallieni thought it expedient to accept these conditions. The guides were received; and by mid-day everything was ready for the march.

In the evening of the same day the caravan reached Dio. Here the same defensive precautions were taken as at Guinina. When the leader sought audience of the chief he found his path barred by a group of natives, who informed him that the king was too old to leave his house, and that he had charged them to receive the white man and treat him with hospitality.

The village itself seemed to contain very few inhabitants, for within the walls almost total silence reigned. These ambassadors of the king, however, seemed disposed to be friendly, assuring the strangers that they had nothing to fear. They promised guides for the morrow, and one of the king's brothers offered himself to accompany the expedition as far as the Niger.

The situation appeared to be becoming less "strained," in diplomatic phrase; but at night, the patrol which Captain Gallieni had despatched to reconnoitre the walls brought back word to the camp that the village, which had appeared to be empty of inhabitants, was, in reality, full of warriors, who were now planning an attack upon the expedition. The crisis was a sufficiently grave one, for every path back to the Senegal was closed to the explorers, and for a little it seemed as if nothing remained but to sell their lives dearly.

Early on the morning of the 11th Captain Gallieni despatched a handsome present to the chief of Dio, and received in turn six large bags of millet, together with the promise of two good guides. Here the five youths of Guinina, who were to accompany the caravan as far as the Niger, informed Captain Gallieni that they were fatigued and wished to return home.

Shortly after mid-day the caravan was in motion, following a straight path for the Baoulé. A deathlike silence reigned around. The village, the forest, the river, all seemed deserted. There was something mysterious and ominous in the intense stillness.

"You'll see, captain," said Barka, the old Senegalee,— "you'll see, something's going to happen."

The stream was crossed without difficulty, and the horsemen were penetrating the forest, every eye on the watch, the muskets slung across the saddle, the

RETREAT OF GALLIENI'S EXPEDITION FROM DIO.

Page 218.

revolvers ready to the hand. Some minutes passed. The guide, under the pretext of avoiding a difficult path for the animals, led the way to the right, through a narrow ravine bounded by lofty and steep slopes. Captain Gallieni felt sure that they had left the right path, and immediately arrested the guide, who, with feigned amazement, threw himself at the leader's feet, and rent the air with his protestations. Barka silenced the fellow's howling at the sword point.

At that moment a discharge of musketry was heard in the direction of the river, and before the echoes had ceased in the forest, a horde of yelling savages were pouring from all sides upon the caravan.

For a moment all was confusion, for the attack was so sudden and at such close quarters that Gallieni's men were unable to use their arms. Presently, however, the spahis and tirailleurs rallied in an open space of ground, and pouring upon their assailants a deadly fire very soon cleared a circle around them. After hard fighting, some ruined battlements which had once formed part of the wall of Dio were gained, and here good vantage-ground was found from which to conduct the defence. The caravan was not a moment too soon in escaping from the deadly *cul-de-sac* into which it had fallen. The enemy continued the attack with shot and spear, but the fire was returned with equal energy. In the first confusion of the surprise, the caravan had got separated into two parts, and the rear, consisting chiefly of the beasts of burden and their conductors, was still close to the river, under the command of Dr. Tautain.

The savages fought fiercely in their native fashion, while Captain Gallieni's men, enraged at the treachery of the Béléris, maintained an indomitable front, obeying the leader's orders with perfect coolness, and exclaiming that they would fight to the last extremity. They threw themselves in front of the leader's horse and covered him with their own bodies! Again and again Barka, leading the spahis, returned from the combat with his sabre red with blood, only to recover breath enough to renew his impetuous onslaught. Captain Gallieni records that his natives showed a courage, on this occasion of terrible odds, worthy of European veterans.

By-and-by, the havoc which followed the fire of Captain Gallieni's men, the courage of the tirailleurs and spahis, the invulnerability which seemed to shield the white men—all this cooled the ardour of the Béléris, and the battle had not lasted more than half an hour, when Captain Gallieni succeeded in cutting a path through the enemy and in rejoining the rear part of the caravan. As they did so, they beheld the interpreter Alassane carrying Dr. Tautain on the croup of his saddle, followed by the survivors of the rear-guard. The doctor had been forced to dismount from his horse early in the fray, the animal having become restive and unmanageable, and had headed his men on foot until the overwhelming numbers of the enemy had compelled him and his little band to retreat.

As rapidly as possible the leaders now began to reorganize the caravan. The most expedient course seemed to be to make for the Niger, which Captain Gallieni hoped by forced marching to reach by the next morning.

Everything was at last ready for the retreat. The dead and wounded, to the number of forty in all, were placed on the horses and mules. The spahis led the caravan under the guidance of Barka, who received orders to strike directly for the east, and to hold on his way through all opposing difficulties. In silence and sadness the march towards the Niger began, through an unknown country, beset with enemies on every side.

The caravan quitted the basin of the Senegal only to enter that of the Niger. As the travellers approached the neighbourhood of the great river, a walled village was sighted, situated at the foot of a range of hills, and a group of natives, watching their herds and surprised at the approach of the caravan.

At the same time it was announced to Captain Gallieni that the Béléris were close behind, and were gathering on the surrounding heights.

What was to be done? It seemed better to approach

the people of this new village, which might possibly belong to the Bammakou country, rather than to risk a second conflict with the Bambarras. Gallieni accordingly drew near the group of natives, which was rapidly increasing in numbers. They sat silent and motionless now, not disturbed by the sight of a white man approaching them alone and unarmed. Through Alassane the interpreter, Captain Gallieni recounted the events of the previous day—the treason of the Bambarras towards a man who was the friend of Bammakou, and who had come to that village as a peace-maker, under the conduct of the son of one of the greatest chiefs of that country.

The natives listened attentively, and at the close of Gallieni's speech assured him that he need fear nothing further at the hands of the Béléris. Then one brought water and another calabashes of native wine, and the white man was reassured.

On the following day the new allies provided guides, the march was resumed, and at mid-day the Niger was beheld afar, rolling through the plain in an easterly direction. But how different was the arrival of the expedition at the great river from what had been hoped for! The caravan was, in truth, in a pitiable plight, deprived of almost all resources and ignorant of what might happen on the morrow.

A little later, Captain Gallieni was met by Albdar-amane, who brought news of Lieutenants Valliere and

Pietri. It must here be explained that Valliere had separated from Gallieni at Kita, and had by this time arrived at Bammakou, where a treaty had been concluded which placed that village under the protectorate of the French.

At one o'clock of the same day Captain Gallieni himself reached Bammakou, where he was met by Pietri and Valliere, who soon placed him in possession of all that had happened since they parted. They had been well received at Bélédougou and at Dio, while at Bammakou their welcome had been of the most sympathetic kind.

The camp was pitched before Bammakou, an important station, whose influence extends throughout all the region of the Upper Niger, from Timbuctoo as far as Tangréla and Sierra Leone. Yet it is no more than a village, occupying an isolated position in a little corner of Bélédougou, with a population of not more than eight hundred.

Since the night of the 8th at Guinina no individual in the camp had closed an eye; the wounded were in a most pitiable condition, some of the men suffering from four or five wounds—rest was indispensable for all. Unfortunately, the reception accorded to Captain Gallieni at Bammakou, unlike that of Valliere and Pietri, was cold in the extreme. The story of the pillage of the expedition at the hands of the Béléris had now reached Bammakou, and the people feared to compromise themselves with the Béléris. To the salutation which Captain Gallieni sent to the chief the latter replied: "A great misfortune has befallen you, for which I can provide no remedy. All I can do is to suffer you to depart with your possessions."

We must here interrupt for a little the story of the main expedition, under the leadership of Captain Gallieni, to give the narrative of Lieutenant Valliere, who separated from Captain Gallieni at Kita for the purpose of exploring the valley of the Bakhoy. This journey was made through a region hitherto unvisited by any European.

The expedition had rested ten days at Kita, and then, while the main body of the caravan directed its march towards the east by way of Bangassi, a small detachment under the command of Lieutenant Valliere took the road to Mourgoula.

After a pretty long stage the village of Goubanko was reached, at the gates of which Lieutenant Valliere was met by a party of men who seemed about to oppose the entrance of himself and his followers. On requesting to be conducted to the chief, Lieutenant Valliere was presented to a number of old men seated on the ground. All were blind, and so old as to have lost the power of articulate speech! To a younger man Valliere explained that his mission was entirely one of peace. The young man thanked the white man simply, and the old chiefs mumbled some confused words of gratitude.

Goubanko is a strongly fortified village, and its inhabitants are an energetic people. Lieutenant Valliere was struck with the fine features of the notables of the place, the paleness of their complexion, and the reserved dignity of their manners. In the evening Captain Gallieni and four spahis entered the camp, and the two white leaders were a little later engaged in a palaver with the people of the village, in which the affairs of Kita were fully discussed. The scene was a curious one. The night had fallen; no light, save that of the stars and what came from two forges hard by, lit up the assembly; and the swarthy forms and faces of the natives gleamed fantastically in the half-light.

The next day Lieutenant Valliere again set out. Khoumo the guide was not to be found, and another had to be obtained in his place. While the little troop was proceeding quietly through a forest, a spahi galloped up to the leader and handed him a letter, the perusal of which explained the enigmatic conduct of Master Khoumo. At Kita the guide had carried off two women, whom he had hidden at Goubanko, which village he had just quitted. This escapade had caused Captain Gallieni considerable annoyance, and he had sent word to Lieutenant Valliere to send back the women.

Khoumo's arrival in camp was sufficiently ludicrous. He was riding at a trot, one of the women before him, the other behind. His ugly face peered comically from under a big straw hat, between the faces of his fair companions. The panting and smoking steed looked as if protesting against his unusual burden, and not quite able to make out the six legs dangling across his back.

Khoumo dismounted amid the laughter of his fellows, followed by the two dusky Helens, silent with astonishment at all that was happening. On Khoumo being ordered to return the two stolen women at once, he answered that he had not stolen them; that he loved Aissé to distraction, and that the other loved him as violently, and would follow him in spite of everything! In the face of the fact that the gallant was of conspicuous ugliness, this statement of the case was extremely ludicrous. Moreover, certain parcels of calico and guinea-cloth which the ladies were carrying tended to put a different complexion upon the story.

Lieutenant Valliere ordered the spahi to take the two women, while Khoumo rent the air with his lamentations, shrieking, "Aissé! Aissé!" Five minutes later, the party having resumed the march, Valliere heard the heart-broken lover explaining in a light tone to his comrades that the captain had acted quite right, and that he (Khoumo) had got his deserts.

Some hours later, when the party were resting in the heat of the day beneath a leafy screen of trees,

Lieutenant Valliere discovered that Khoumo had again vanished. At mid-day he reappeared covered with dust and perspiration. He had followed the spahi and Aissé, and suborned the former to give up his lady-love. Valliere peremptorily ordered Khoumo to say where he had hidden Aissé a second time. The rascal stammered and hesitated, and then called "Aissé!" who presently issued from her hiding-place, a few yards from the camp. The spahi once more took possession of the woman; while Khoumo, giving way to a fit of passion, refused to accompany the party any longer, caught up a gun, and threatened to shoot any one who approached him. He was seized and disarmed, and it was made plain to him that if he tried to escape he would be at once shot.

In the afternoon Lieutenant Valliere quitted Bammakou, and directed his course for the lagoon of Delaba, but soon found his march obstructed by a succession of pools forming a channel now almost dry. The guide informed him that they had reached Delaba, and the leader decided to camp here. Towards nightfall a violent wind arose, the lightning flashed, and a thunder-clap split a lemon-tree close to the camp. The party were wholly without shelter, and were presently exposed to the full fury of a tornado of unusual violence. The dust enveloped them in a whirlwind, while their faces and hands were literally whipped by the pebbles which the fury of the storm raised. The men durst open neither eyes nor mouth for fear of being blinded or stifled, and all thought with dread of the long night before them. The rain had already begun, and a night of exposure to tropical rain often means a fever next day.

Fortunately, the tornado was as short-lived as it was furious; the rain came to nothing. The storm was of a sort characteristic of these latitudes towards the approach of the winter season.

On the same evening Lieutenant Valliere received a letter from Captain Gallieni by the hands of a native porter, and set out next morning, hoping to reach Mourgoula the same day. The march led first through a beautiful forest country, and afterwards across great expanses covered with small stones, and presenting the curious appearance of having been rained upon by a thick shower of pebbles.

At two o'clock Sitakoto was reached, and a party of negroes met with—caravans from the Upper Niger, as usual, with a train of male and female slaves; a miserable sight, from which the white leader was glad to turn away his eyes.

The party were extremely wearied with a long day's march, and Valliere's temples throbbed so violently that for a little he feared he had received a sunstroke. By keeping his head for a little time in a bucket of cold water, however, the pain was alleviated.

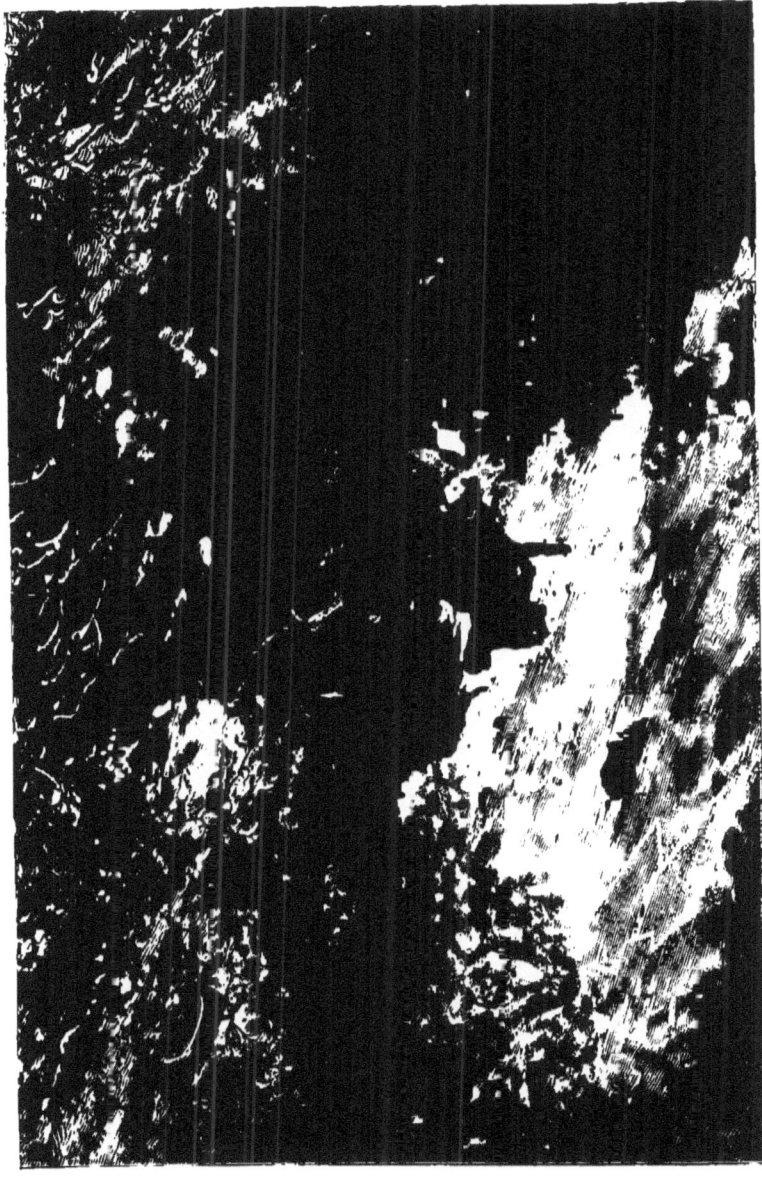

TORNADO IN THE BIRGO COUNTRY.

Page 229.

The chief of Sitakoto arrived presently, and declared himself honoured by a visit from the white man; and regretted that, owing to his poverty, he could not give him a fitting reception. All Lieutenant Valliere said he wished was provisions for his party, for which he would amply pay. Millet proved very scarce, and was only procurable at double the usual price.

Late in the afternoon Mourgoula was reached. A tall Toucouleur, of forbidding aspect, requested Lieutenant Valliere to follow him. The white man was then informed that Almamy could not receive him at present, and that he was at liberty to camp where he chose.

Next morning Almamy still refused to see the white leader. Valliere told the chief that it was the governor of St. Louis's business, and that he could only set out again with regret that he had not seen Almamy. This had the desired effect: the chief commanded the white man's presence.

Five or six grave personages were squatted round the king, who occupied a clean hut, and sat on a carpet of sheep-skins. An empty bench was placed for Lieutenant Valliere to sit on, and a sabre was laid at his feet. Almamy wore a mask which covered all his face except the eyes, and his head was adorned with a large turban. Valliere saluted him, explained the object of the mission, and gave him a letter from the governor of Senegal. Almamy demanded why Kita and Goubanko had been reconciled without his being consulted. Was he not the territorial chief of the country?

This brusque reception surprised Valliere a good deal; but he tried to show Almamy that Captain Gallieni had acted with all honourable intentions in arbitrating between the two villages. Almamy now read the letter, and his face cleared somewhat.

"The governor of St. Louis speaks well. Thou art going to Amadou. Be welcome. I am only the eye of my master."

The chief then offered a guide; and on Lieutenant Valliere requesting that a courier should be sent forward with a letter of explanation, consented. Finally, the white leader quitted Almamy on the best of terms, having presented him with a gun and a handsome mantle, while his wives received bottles of scent, jewelry, etc.

In the evening Almamy returned his guest's visit. He was now unmasked, and revealed a face of amiable aspect, with soft eyes. Was this the ferocious tyrant of report? Almamy had surely the gift of masking his countenance when he chose in more senses than one. The chief thanked the white man for his present, as did his daughter on bended knees.

When Lieutenant Valliere had quitted the village, he learned that Almamy had secretly hesitated about allowing him to continue his journey: thus skilful are the Toucouleurs in the art of dissimulation.

After a difficult march the travellers reached Koukouroni. Lieutenant Valliere found the inhabitants a poor and miserable people, who had suffered severely at the hands of the Toucouleurs. They gathered about the white strangers in attitudes of the utmost humility, and when a gun was discharged thought it witchcraft. The camp was visited by a little girl of such conspicuous beauty that Lieutenant Valliere transmitted her graceful form and charming face to the pages of his sketch-book. She had very beautiful, soft, and dreamy eyes, shining hair crowned with a coronet of glass beads, while her figure was the personification of natural grace. The poor people were dumb with astonishment at the approximate likeness which Valliere succeeded in catching of the little Koukouroni beauty.

On the 2nd of May the party reached Niagakoura, a miserable village with some hundred inhabitants, situated in the middle of a desert. After a long and weary march through a hot and stony country, the travellers at length camped beside a beautiful little river, thrice welcome after the excessive heat of the journey. A more favourable camping-ground could not be desired than under the cool shadow of the trees that bordered the stream. A bath refreshed the weary travellers, and a dish of perch from the river made a welcome change for supper.

The region through which Lieutenant Valliere was

now travelling receives the general name of Birgo—a well-watered and fertile country, containing but a scanty population. The people wear little clothing—the women wearing a girdle only, and the children going entirely naked. The agricultural products of the country are chiefly maize and millet and a little cotton. No oxen are seen anywhere, and only a very few sheep and goats. Butter-trees abound; the people gathering only enough of the fruit to serve their immediate wants. The people have abandoned hunting. Although one of the chief commercial roads of West Soudan crosses the country, it leads to no trade with these people, who are too poor to buy cloth, and are limited to the exchange of glass beads and such like for provisions with the passing caravans. The natives are among the best favoured physically of the Soudan tribes, and the country possesses many natural advantages. Their miserable condition is due to the baneful rule of the Toucouleurs. When this is replaced by a milder and more beneficent government, prosperity and happiness may yet return to Birgo.

Lieutenant Valliere quitted with regret the beautiful camp, and, resuming the march, reached the walled village of Niagassola, a considerable place, with a population of one thousand. Valliere presented himself to the king, and explained as usual the object of the mission. The chief, an old man of tall and stalwart aspect, replied that the stranger was welcome, and that his ancestors had ever treated the white man with hospitality.

Three days' march to the south of Niagassola lies Bouré, a little republic governed by the heads of four families. An industrious people, little given to war, occupy the country in security and peace. Lieutenant Vallière visited Bouré, and was received by the reigning prince with much circumstance and ceremony, which, intended to be impressive, was not a little comical. After a good deal of preliminary state etiquette, the white leader was permitted to shake hands with the aged chief, whom he subsequently presented with a beautiful rifle.

On the 5th of May the party reached Koumakhana, situated in an important gold country, whose mines constitute the entire wealth of the people. The natives work the mines wholly with the pick. When the workmen have reached a certain depth they draw up the siftings in calabashes attached to cords; and in order to facilitate their descent into the mines, they cut holes in the walls for their hands and feet.

The neighbouring pools supply the facilities for washing the gold. The more delicate operation of washing the mineral is intrusted to the women. The auriferous earth, having been extracted from the mine, is placed in calabashes filled with clear water. The workers keep the calabashes moving in a circle, and gradually the quartz, separating itself from the gravel, falls to the bottom of the vessel. Lieutenant Valliere was anxious to learn how much gold was thus purified and made into ingots, but the Koumakhana miners refused to give him any idea.

Continuing his journey, Valliere and his comrades arrived at a broad plateau bounded by the mountains of Manding, stretching east and by south; and shortly after the important village of Naréna, with its two large gates, was reached.

Report credited the people of Naréna with being little given to hospitality, and Lieutenant Valliere was able to add his testimony to the same effect. He was, in truth, but brusquely received by the chief, and deemed it expedient to waste as little time as possible in his territory.

Shortly after quitting Naréna, the party gained the banks of the beautiful river Amarakoba, whose golden waters, flowing over their rocky bed, wander on to join the main river. The travellers were here followed by a caravan of slaves, composed almost entirely of children, who, entirely ignorant of the fate awaiting them, played and gambolled about—bathing in the river, chasing the fish and insects, and filling the air with their shouts and laughter. Lieutenant Valliere gathered from the leader of the caravan many particulars regarding his hateful trade. These files of slaves, gathered from all parts of Soudan, were to feed the markets of the Upper Niger, where they were sold to the Moors of Sahara. The profits accruing from the trade are considerable.

On the day following the meeting with the slave-caravan, the explorers arrived at Mana-Oulé, a very singular natural conformation, composed of a mountain presenting a succession of vertical terraced walls, bastioned, as it were, by all sorts of rocky towers, which give it the appearance of a gigantic piece of mason-work. A little further on Nienkema was reached, built at the foot of a picturesque mass of rocks; while a short distance off rose two lofty obelisks, formed of graystone. These singular pinnacles inclined forward at so sharp an angle that they looked as if threatening at every moment to overwhelm the unlucky village at their base. The attention of Lieutenant Valliere was arrested by many curiously-shaped rocks in this neighbourhood; some like vast colonnades, others like gates and porches, all of most odd and unexpected appearance.

The village of Sibi was next sighted, and the leader was pushing on with some impatience to reach it, for his men were fatigued with the march and the heat, when he was arrested by symptoms of extreme fear on the part of the guide, who was eagerly listening in the direction of the village, while at the same time urging silence in the camp. What was up now? thought the leader.

Lieutenant Valliere now listened in turn, and

thought he heard cries in the distance, repeated at short intervals. The guide declared that it would not be advisable to approach the village to-day, for that these cries betokened the *komou*. The interpreter could not very well explain what that meant, but spoke of sorceries and *fêtes* and "beasts of Malinkés." Lieutenant Valliere, impatient at the delay, pushed on, convinced that there was nothing to fear—Sori, the tirailleurs, and the muleteers alone following. The guide and the caravan remained where they were, overcome by terror.

As the lieutenant and his followers drew near Sibi, the cries became more distinct. The voices of both young and old people were heard mingling in a sort of wailing, plaintive as the mountain echoes dying away in space. At length, after turning a small clump of trees, Vallicre encountered a young Mandingue carrying a calabash containing meal and a chicken. The boy uttered a prolonged cry, and running up to the strangers, made strenuous gestures with the object of arresting their further progress. But the sun was beating down on the heads of the travellers, and a broad-shadowed bread-fruit tree at the gate of the village invited rest. No power on earth could have prevented the leader at that moment from seeking the protection of its leafy boughs.

The cause of the commotion was the komou, a religious festival which precedes the sowing of the seed.

The Mandingues, like all the Bambarras of the Upper Niger, are given over to fetich-worship. Each village has its sacred grove, impenetrable except by a path barred with thorny branches. Here, in the mysterious shade, is held the terrible rite which is the master of the destiny of the village and its inhabitants. The village attempts no enterprise of any hazard without consulting the wishes of the fetich. If the people are about to make war, a kid is sacrificed, its blood is sprinkled on the sacred stones, and by certain signs the sacrificing priest interprets the decisions of the fetich. Then the warriors march to battle with confidence.

In the same way, at the approach of seed-time they sacrifice to the god in order to obtain a good sprouting of the grain; then comes the *fête*, which is to insure a good harvest; and lastly, when the granaries are full, another visit to the sacred wood is made, to get the assurance that no enemy will have part or lot in the harvests of the year. The influence of this superstition makes itself felt throughout the whole social life of the people; and the young woman who desires a prosperous marriage offers her sacrifice of eggs, or a measure of meal, or any other gift which she thinks will be agreeable to the great dispenser of all gifts.

It is only the male population who have the right of approaching the sacred grove, and since early morning on the day when Lieutenant Valliere arrived at Sibi, they had been rending the air with their cries, with the object of drawing down the fetich into the thicket.

It will readily be understood how the arrival of the strangers interrupted this solemn festival; but the old man made a path for the white leader. "Understand," exclaimed one, "that this white man is the first who has visited our country; and remark, too, that he has come, not upon an ordinary day, but in the very midst of the komou. Is not the intention of the fetich evident?" And thus the situation of the strangers, so menacing in the morning, became more favourable.

With the object of propitiating the notables of the village, Lieutenant Valliere prepared a box of yellow cloths, which excited universal admiration; probably no such fine stuffs had ever been seen in Sibi. The old chief remarked, that the good omen of the white man's arrival at this particular season was already beginning to bear fruits, and that the present komou would be the most memorable in his reign.

The *fête* was completely absorbing the whole population, and Lieutenant Valliere was able to note its curious details. Towards noon the cries had ceased, and every man, still carrying his calabash of millet and chicken, was directing his steps towards the sacred wood. There the groups formed themselves in silence, and at a given signal all at once raised a great shout. Then the old priests entered the thicket and began the sacrifice. It was not possible for the spectators to witness the vast hecatombs of chickens which then took place within the wood.

Both old and young men, in a sort of wild delirium, then began a strange and excited dance, every one striving to twist and contort himself as much as possible. The dance continued during the whole time the sacrifices within the wood were going on. There was no pause, no intermission; many dropped down breathless on the ground. At last the priests, the holocaust finished, emerged from the wood. Then there was a sort of assembly held, at the conclusion of which all returned to the village with their empty calabashes.

Presently everybody returned, carrying dry branches, and walked in a procession along the path leading to the wood. Arrived there, the crowd collected before the entrance, and every one began violently beating the ground, at the same time uttering loud cries. The object of this last ceremony was, it appeared, to get the fetich to depart.

For a short space tranquillity succeeded these noisy manifestations; but the sacred part of the programme fairly finished, abundant drinking and feasting followed. The place which the revellers chose for their merry-making was the beautiful tree under which Lieutenant Valliere and his little band were encamped. The Lieutenant deemed it prudent to seek the intervention of the chief, who presently appeared, very much the worse for his deep potations, and stammered out a speech which in no wise tended to silence the uproar going on around. A sort of fury began to take possession of the crowd, and a general riot seemed imminent.

The tipsy old chief began to weep, at which several of his subjects strove to console and sustain him. The scene became more and more tumultuous, and at last Lieutenant Vallicre was obliged to draw his revolver and threaten the crowd. But by-and-by the groups began to disperse themselves over the plain and give themselves up to their various diversions.

On the following morning the travellers resumed the march without much regret, and arrived next at Nafadié, the chief of which came to meet them—an immense man with a great jolly face. He entertained the white man hospitably, and provided a sheep for his followers. Nafadié is a village with a population of about seven hundred.

One of the villagers told Lieutenant Valliere that he had seen a white man, and the leader did not doubt but that it was one of the officers of the expedition. He asked the man to describe Bammakou, and he replied, as others had done, that it was a beautiful village, whose leading men were very wealthy. This was a pleasant prospect after the desert and the miserable villages of Manding.

Lieutenant Valliere's further journey was undisturbed and uneventful. He quitted Nafadié after making liberal presents to the chief, who received them with every manifestation of delight, while the women prostrated themselves on the ground in token of thanks.

Between Nafadié and Bammakou the road skirts the mountains of Manding, and the Niger. The path is well defined and easy. No obstacles were encountered, except five small streams, which were easily crossed. The last of these—the Balanke—passed, the travellers journeyed on with the joy of men whose labours and fatigues were over and who were about to rejoin their friends. On the following day Bammakou was reached. Here a considerable disappointment awaited the leader.

After all the flattering accounts of Bammakou which he had received from time to time from natives, he expected to find a large town, an important commercial centre. The neighbourhood of an African market is usually a bustling and animated scene enough; the approaches are full of traders going and coming. But here there was nothing of all this—nothing but the profoundest solitude. Lieutenant Valliere was told that this state of things was due to wars with the Toucouleurs; but this did not seem altogether to explain the almost absolute want of life in the place.

But another question soon absorbed Lieutenant Valliere. Where was the mission? With its numerous following, it would have been certain to give life to the neighbourhood. The lieutenant's surprise gave place to apprehension. Putting his horse to the gallop he approached the gate of the village; but there he was stopped by a native, who motioned to him mysteriously. This reception increased his anxiety; but he was presently reassured by the sight of Lieutenant Pietri. In a few words he was made aware of the situation. Bammakou was now nothing more than a big village, ruined by war, and without commercial importance. As to Captain Gallieni and his followers, they were still to arrive, and Pietri had had no communication with them for many days. Rumours of the intended attack upon the mission had arrived, however; and as no word of their comrades reached Valliere and Pietri during the evening, they were filled with anxiety. Their anxious forebodings were sufficiently realized, for next day they were to learn the misfortune which had overtaken and all but annihilated the expedition.

We now take up again Captain Gallieni's narrative at the point at which we left it—the arrival of the expedition at Bammakou, and the reunion with Lieutenant Valliere. The chief of Bammakou received the mission hospitably, Valliere having prepared the way. The caravan was in a most deplorable condition, destitute of provisions, of medicines, and of presents for the tribes. The men were wounded, sick, and weary; arms had been lost and ammunition exhausted. With very anxious hearts the reunited leaders took counsel together, when Captain Gallieni proposed to push on the march in the face of everything. Officers and men alike supported the leader in his resolution, and it was determined to continue the journey.

But it had become a pressing need that despatches should be sent to St. Louis. Dr. Bayol, whose special duties in connection with the expedition might now be considered over, offered to make the journey back to St. Louis alone, with Sori, the interpreter, as a guide. The doctor took with him a full and exact written account of the attack upon the mission at Dio and all that followed thereupon, which he was to deliver into the hands of the governor. He was then to send on as rapidly as possible a supply of medicines for the caravan, whose stock was now reduced to thirty grains of quinine, and the winter season already close at hand.

Captain Gallieni also sent back the ass-drivers, who were of no further service, and who simply terrified by their uncouth and miserable appearance the tribes through which the caravan passed. It was with regret that the leader took this step, for the poor fellows had shown themselves faithful and even devoted in his service. They were liberally recompensed for their labours and fatigues, and commended to the attention of the governor of St. Louis in a letter to be delivered by Dr. Bayol.

The expedition resumed the march, and on the 15th of May reached the village of Joliba — Dr. Bayol meanwhile taking the route to Kita, the party of ass-drivers in his wake. Pietri and Alassane preceded the caravan to the banks of the river in order to make preparations for the crossing. An hour's march across a wide grassy plain brought the explorers to the banks of the great river of Soudan. It was with feelings of emotion that Captain Gallieni and his comrades gazed upon the mighty water-course. The banks were of no great height, but the river rolled between them, its immense volume of water and numerous islands dotting its surface giving to it a picturesque and imposing appearance. The travellers crossed the ford in canoes, small, leaky craft, that took in water at all sides. The horses and mules, held by the spahis who were seated in the canoes, crossed by swimming.

By five o'clock men and animals were on the other side of the Joliba, where the mission was favourably received by a party of Toucouleurs, one of whom, a man with an intelligent face, advanced towards the leader, and having made the customary *salaam*, spoke thus :—

"The country is yours, and you are at home, since you come as ambassadors to the sultan of Ségou. We know the powerful chief who has sent you, and my master, who rules over this village in the name of Amadou, will be happy to receive you. He sends me to you to say, 'Bismillah!' You have left your native land and encountered many toils; but now all that is over. You are at home. 'Bismillah! bismillah!'"

These were agreeable words to listen to after the brutal reception of the expedition at the hands of the Bambarras of Bélédougou. The mission quickly arrived at Toniella, and passed through the gates. Huts were placed at the service of Captain Gallieni and his followers; chickens, rice, and butter were provided for the men, and corn for the horses. The hearts of the travel-worn white men were filled with pleasurable emotions by this amicable reception.

The travellers lay down to sleep on their mats in peace and security; but, alas! all the night their slumbers were broken by the barking of dogs, the noise of the tom-tom, and the shouting and singing of tipsy Bambarras, who were speeding the night with deep potations of dolo.

On the following morning Captain Gallieni took advantage of the friendly attitude of his hosts to consult with them about the wounded, who were no longer able to support the fatigues of the journey. The people agreed to receive and tend the sick men, who were to rejoin the caravan when they were again in a condition to travel. In return for this service the leader left behind him a number of guns to pay for the board and care of the wounded.

The march now led towards the east, under the conduct of a guide. The country traversed was exceedingly fertile, watered by the Niger and its chief affluents. The land produces abundance of maize, rice, cotton, tobacco, indigo, and millet, while vast forests of butter-trees abound—a magnificent territory awaiting European settlement and improved cultivation. In addition to its agricultural resources the district is, moreover, rich in minerals.

The village of Cissina was reached. Shortly after the arrival of the expedition at this point the white men witnessed a Bambarra funeral. First came a score of women weeping violently. Next two griots— one with a small tom-tom chanted the praises of the departed. Then came the corpse, carried by six men in a finely-woven net. Last followed the parents and friends of the dead man, armed with guns. The Bambarras always bury their dead close to their villages, the chiefs being interred in their own huts. While the earth is being thrown upon the corpse, all the friends of the dead man make believe of being buried in the tomb with him.

Tadiana was the next halt, an important Toucouleur fort, with a population partly of Bambarras, partly of Sarracolets. On the night of the 17th of May the mission reached Diba, where they were met by a party of Bambarras, who examined the strangers closely by the light of their torches, touching their hands and faces to assure themselves that they were white men.

On the following day Kobilé was reached—a small village of some three hundred inhabitants. Here corn was procured for the horses, and the chief himself brought a sheep for the strangers, while his brother offered a chicken, saying :—

"I give you this chicken. Were I rich and powerful I should give you a much finer present; but as I am neither rich nor powerful, I cannot entertain as you deserve—a people so important as you—and I much regret the smallness of my gift."

The white men were provided with a good hut, the walls of which were very curious, being covered with hieroglyphics, while from the roof were suspended amulets, castanets, etc. But the most curious object in the collection was a sword, evidently of European make, bearing this legend : "Never draw me without cause : never sheathe me without honour." The weapon bore the appearance of being of very ancient manufacture.

On the 19th the expedition crossed the Faya, an important affluent of the Niger, and arrived at Niagué, a village of some five hundred inhabitants. After halting at several intermediate stages the travellers reached Sanankoro. Here they rested the best part of a day, the leaders passing the time in speculation as to how far they might still be from Ségou, which seemed to get further and further off every day. Here Amadou at last gave some sign of his existence, for Alpha came to announce that two men from the Toucouleur capital had arrived and requested to speak with Captain Gallieni.

They were introduced, and proved to be two Sofas. They said that they were come from the sultan to inform the white leader that he was to remain where they, the envoys, found him; in whatever village he might be, there he was to stay for the meantime.

Captain Gallieni protested energetically against this, saying that two months had been consumed in the march; and was the mission to be detained in a small village, deprived of all resources, and the winter rains setting in, blotting out the paths and preventing all access to the capital? The two Sofas answered, that they were simply transmitting the orders of Lam Dioulbé. Those orders were clear and formulated: they, the envoys, were to arrest the mission wherever they met it. They knew, moreover, that Sanankoro could not supply sufficient food for the men and horses of the expedition. The white leaders should push on to Niansonnah, a richer village, and there await the answer of the sultan.

Captain Gallieni then told the emissaries that he had written a letter in Arabic which he wished to send to Amadou by Lieutenant Pietri, accompanied by the interpreter Alpha Sega. No objection was made to this, the men answering that Amadou would send some of his chief men to receive the white man's communications.

Sanankoro was left on the 24th, Niamana was passed, and the camp pitched at Niansonnah, which was found to be a far less prosperous place than the two Sofas had reported. It was with great difficulty that enough food was obtained to sustain the caravan for four days. On the 29th Captain Gallieni summoned the two Sofas and informed them that as no reply had yet come from Amadou, the expedition was about to quit the village and resume the journey. Seeing that it would be useless to try to detain the caravan further, the two men decided to take themselves off, satisfied of the consequences that would ensue from this disobedience of the sultan's orders.

Resuming the march, the expedition reached Dindian, and Soïa, and, after traversing a wide plain, Nango. Here the travellers were met by a party of twelve horsemen, who escorted them to the village, where huts had been provided for the accommodation of the leaders. About mid-day Captain Gallieni sought an interview with Marico, the chief of the village, who, after the customary salaam, spoke thus:—

"I was at Ségou when Amadou was informed of your arrival. He at once ordered me to depart in order to receive you. I was to make you welcome, and to provide food for your men and animals. You, for your part, were to remain here at Nango, to await the answer of the sultan. Lam Dioulbé knows all that has happened to you. In regard to the wrong you have suffered, it is for him to avenge you. You are the ambassadors of a powerful chief, and you shall be treated accordingly."

All this was very fine, but it was not exactly the point. Captain Gallieni tried to make Marico comprehend that the mission was at its last extremity, that men and animals could do no more, and that after all the expedition had suffered, even such short delays as this prejudiced the march. Marico replied tranquilly that he was but transmitting the orders of Amadou, and that he was about to depart for Ségou at moonrise, to seek the will of his master.

Marico accordingly departed, and returned in a day or two. He did not give Captain Gallieni much satisfaction by the news he brought, for he declared that Amadou advised the white man to bear in mind, when he felt impatient, that he was travelling through a stranger's country, and should therefore submit to the wishes of the chief of that country, who would presently send two envoys to treat with the white man.

On the 5th June these two ambassadors duly made their appearance. They were Samba N'Diaye, the chief engineer of the sultan, and Boubakar Saada, a notable of Amadou's court. The two ambassadors spoke much to the same effect as the Sofa men had previously done—promises on the part of Amadou mingled with half-threats. Captain Gallieni resolved to send back to the sultan, by Samba N'Diaye and Boubakar, an exact statement of his position and complaints. The envoys returned in a day or two, bringing the same vague words—promises and interdicts which always composed Amadou's answers, and against which it was useless and even dangerous on the part of the white men to do more than remonstrate.

At last Amadou promised to send one of his chief ministers to make a treaty with the mission; and after much delay and time wasted, this meeting did at length take place. On the 13th of October, Seïdou Diéylia, Amadou's prime minister, arrived at Nango with great pomp and a large following. The negotiations lasted for nearly a week, and after interminable discussion Captain Gallieni obtained from Seïdou a deed placing the Niger under French protectorate, from its source as far as Timbuctoo. On the 3rd November the treaty, drawn up in French and Arabic, was signed by all the parties concerned, except by Amadou himself. Seïdou was to take the document to Ségou for the sultan to sign, and promised Captain Gallieni that this would be done in the course of a few days.

The few days lengthened themselves out into weeks and then into months, and still the treaty remained unsigned by the sultan. Every possible pretext which the wily Mussulman could devise for delaying to append his sign-manual to the document, without which it was valueless, was brought forward. Those at the court who were wholly unfriendly to the mission, alleged that its object was not to conclude a commercial and friendly treaty, but to make plans of the country, to establish European colonies, and to enlist the hostile tribes of Bambarras and Malinkes against the sultan. To these advisers Amadou was only too ready to listen.

The mission spent weary months at Nango. One after the other the four white men were attacked by fever, and lay ill and weak in the midst of a strange and hostile country. The food that could be obtained was poor and insufficient; and over and above these physical troubles, there was the daily mental anxiety and worry, the daily deferred hope that Amadou would keep his word and allow the mission to depart. The horses died too, and unless Amadou supplied their places, how should the travellers be able to accomplish their return journey?

But at last Amadou, urged by the reiterated demands of Captain Gallieni, placed his signature to the treaty and told the mission to prepare for departure. With indescribable joy the white men began to get everything ready for the return march—to prepare means of transport, to repair clothes for the journey, and re-equip the caravan as speedily and as well as was possible in the circumstances.

It was not until the 10th of March that Amadou returned the treaty signed to Captain Gallieni. A few days after, he sent five good horses, three oxen for carrying the baggage, and a supply of rice, meal, salt, and other provisions; and besides this, a present of gold, and twenty pieces of cloth of Ségou workmanship. On the arrival of the expedition at St Louis, the gold was distributed among the interpreters of the mission. Thus, in a measure, Amadou made up for the delay, anxiety, sickness, and general wretchedness which he had for many months caused the mission to suffer.

On the 21st March 1881, Nango opened its gates to allow the expedition to depart. The poor people of the village had done their best to treat the white men kindly, and the whole population followed them outside the gates, crying, "Bonjour, Toubab! Bonjour, Toubab!" Captain Gallieni and his companions did not depart without leaving behind them many little souvenirs among the simple village people.

The return journey led along the Niger, the route followed being very much the same as the previous one. Kantara, one of Amadou's chief agents, was charged with the convoy of the expedition as far as Tourella.

On the 22nd March the village of Sougoulani

was reached. Here the travellers were the witnesses of a dreadful spectacle. Amadou, with the characteristic cruelty of the Mussulmans, had ordered a number of prisoners of war to be put to death, with the object of inspiring terror among the neighbouring tribes; and now Captain Gallieni and his comrades beheld the bodies of these victims heaped up in the village market-place, the prey of hyenas and birds—a veritable human shambles. An entire caravan, consisting of sixteen persons, of all ages and both sexes, had been captured by Amadou's emissaries and pitilessly put to death. As the white men rode past this sad and horrible spectacle, they could not but reflect on the danger to which they had been exposed at Nango, living so long at the mercy of the fickle and sombre tyrant of Ségou.

On the 27th the journey proved full of difficulties, the passage of the little river Faya alone delaying the caravan an hour. The river was fringed with beautiful fig-trees, whose branches projected far over the water. Some of the men entered the stream to help in getting the animals and baggage across. Others scrambled across along the stems and branches of the trees, some of which extended right across the river. The leaders adopted this method of crossing, and the party swarming along the boughs from bank to bank looked ludicrously like a troop of monkeys.

On the 28th Tadiana was reached, and a halt of

an hour made. The chief, Daba, confirmed the news, which had already reached the leaders of the expedition, of the arrival of a French force at Kita. Daba spoke of the astonishing effect which this event had produced upon the surrounding tribes, the turbulent Talibés being struck dumb with amazement.

The march was resumed across a plain very much cut up by the rains, and the bivouac was made at Cissina, in a splendid hut formed of bamboos and the stalks of the millet. Here an agreeable day was spent by the travellers, who awaited the morrow in the pleasant anticipation of reaching the other bank of the Niger. The hut was visited by crowds of the natives, curious to see the white men, who, they believed, had been abandoned to death by the tyrant sultan, but whom the latest reports had surrounded with fame.

Tourella was reached on the 29th March. Here Captain Gallieni parted with his remaining stock of cowries to the chief, Kantara. Valliere proceeded in advance, to announce the arrival of the party at Nagadie. Kantara gave the leaders a number of particulars in regard to the eventful battle at Dio, from which it appeared that the Bambarras had suffered severely. They had, in a word, reaped the just reward of their treachery and ingratitude; and the result of the conflict, severely as the mission itself had suffered, had inspired the attackers with a wholesome dread of the white men. Towards noon of the same day the caravan reached the banks of the river, where canoes were in readiness for the passage across. The party embarked in the midst of a great crowd of negroes, gathered from all the surrounding villages. Some natives, who had accompanied the white men from Ségou, were concealed among Captain Gallieni's own followers, with the design of crossing to the right bank of the Niger. These endeavoured to embark in the canoes; but the watchful Kantara was on the outlook for all such. Among these poor people was one old Ouoloff woman who had lost her husband in one of the raids of Amadou, and who now wished to rejoin her husband. The white men interceded in her case, but Kantara was inflexible. It was as much as his life was worth to listen to her entreaties, and it was in vain that the poor old creature rent the air with her cries, offering to serve as a slave to the white men if she might only go with them.

In the space of two hours the whole caravan were on the opposite bank of the Niger. It was a curious sight to see the men, both Toucouleurs and Bambarras, uniting to take a firm resolution that this was the last time they should ever accept hospitality from Amadou. Previously these poor people had had a great belief and confidence in the generosity, the magnificence, and the omnipotence of the son of El

Hadj. But their six months' sojourn at Nango, with its unceasing anxieties of every sort, had quite disillusioned them on this score, and proved to them beyond all doubt how wretched the life of Amadou's subjects was compared with that of the tribes along the Senegal placed under the French protectorate.

The march was resumed in the direction of Nafadié, across an extensive grassy plain. As the caravan approached the village of Joliba, a crowd of people was perceived in the distance gathered under some bread-fruit trees. Captain Gallieni's anxiety was raised to behold Lieutenant Valliere stretched motionless on the ground at the foot of a tree, with two or three natives beside him endeavouring by means of vigorous friction to revive him. In a few minutes more, Gallieni, Pietri, and Tautain were at the side of their comrade, who presently opened his eyes. The doctor then examined him, and, to the great relief of all, discovered that he was not hurt in any way.

Valliere thus narrated the cause of his present situation:—After quitting Joliba in the morning, he was deserted by his guides, and left to his own resources. He chose a path which, as he thought, led to Nafadié, but which in reality led to the mountains. After many turnings and detours, he at length came upon a village situated in a narrow and rugged gorge. It appeared that that same morning a party of Toucouleur horsemen had made a raid upon this village, and carried off a number of young girls who were watching the flocks. The inhabitants mistook Valliere and his companions for a part of these robbers, and forthwith attacked him. Some of the tirailleurs who accompanied him were made prisoners, and one was seriously wounded. Valliere himself escaped the bullets of his pursuers, which whistled about his ears, and reached Joliba again half dead with hunger and fatigue. Before the day ended, however, the lieutenant had recovered, and was able to resume the journey.

The people of Nafadié gave the mission a hospitable reception, providing mutton, rice, and couscous in abundance. Gallieni took advantage of the friendly attitude of the inhabitants to demonstrate to them the pacific intentions of the whites, and how necessary it was that the chiefs of Nafadié should unite against Amadou, whose troopers were constantly carrying off their women and harrying their flocks. The reply of the chiefs was unanimous. They were perfectly willing to place themselves under the French protectorate, and to break through the intolerable domination of the Toucouleurs. Captain Gallieni then unfolded to them the plan of the treaty, and the notables of the village forthwith affixed their signatures to the document.

On the 30th of March, the caravan took the road for Tabou, halting at Kamalia, Sibi, and Nienkema, in order that the signatures of the chiefs of these villages might be obtained to the treaty. Captain Gallieni's task was now a light one, Amadou being cordially detested throughout all this region. The tribes appeared perfectly satisfied to see the whites established at Makadiambougou. A day was spent at Tabou, where the inhabitants, notwithstanding their simple savagedom, offered the mission every hospitality,. providing corn, water, wood, etc. This village absolutely hangs, as it were, on the flank of the mountain, guarded by huge blocks of stone, a natural protection against the raids of Toucouleur troopers.

On the 31st, Naréna was reached, a large Malinké village, whose chief received the white men courteously, though he had treated Valliere in a considerably more rough and ready fashion some months previously. An ox was presented to the leaders, and the people disputed among themselves as to who should entertain the men of the expedition. The treaty was signed with enthusiasm, and Captain Gallieni now felt sure that Sultan Amadou might regard as lost all the provinces in the valley of the Bakhoy.

At Naréna, Captain Gallieni received precise news as to what had been occurring at Kita. Two messengers arrived from Lieutenant-Colonel Borgnis-Desbordes, whose anxiety had been great on account of the mission, the arrival of which he waited for with eagerness.

Naréna was quitted next day, and a short halt made at Koremakhava, whose chief joined the alliance. Niagassola was reached on April 2nd, whence Captain Gallieni despatched a letter to Kita to announce his arrival. A parley was held with the chief of the ancient village of Bangassi, which the expedition had found deserted and in ruins a year before, and whose inhabitants were for the most part refugees from Niagassola and the neighbourhood. Captain Gallieni spoke of the era of peace and prosperity which awaited all the tribes of this region upon the settlement of the whites at Kita, and engaged to repeople the village of Bangassi.

After leaving Niagassola, Captain Gallieni presented the treaty for signature to the chief, Mambi, who showed himself very anxious that his village should be chosen as the site of the French colony that was to be established between Kita and the Niger.

The 3rd of April was passed at the little village of Koukouroni, whose chief, a handsome old man of somewhat sad bearing, apologized for not being able to welcome the mission in a more hospitable fashion. The Toucouleurs had robbed him of everything. The white leader endeavoured to reassure and console the old chief, and presented him with a small sum of money.

On the following day the caravan rested at Mourgoula, where the white men were received with much ceremony. Towards mid-day Captain Gallieni received a letter from Lieutenant-Colonel Borgnis-Desbordes, which conveyed a gracious welcome, and expressed with what impatience the arrival of the mission at Kita was looked forward to. Mourgoula was quitted in the evening, and the night passed at Sitakoto. At Goubanko the travellers were received by MM. de Gasquet and Morlot, whom the governor of the colony had sent to meet them.

A great change had passed over the country since the setting out of the expedition a year back. The French flag now floated on the fort that had been raised near Makadiambougou, and the French influence extended over a wide area of the Niger basin.

The envoy of the Sultan Amadou was unable to conceal his surprise at finding the white men so firmly established within so short a distance of Mourgoula, one of his own possessions.

On the 16th of April the expedition arrived at the confluence of the Bafing and the Bakhoy, where, on the right bank of the former river, a military post was established.

On the 23rd, Bakel was reached. Here boats were procured to transport the members of the expedition as far as Podor. On the 27th the mission found itself in an enemy's country. The river-side natives showed themselves exceedingly hostile, attempting to arrest the passage of the boats down the river. The leaders of the expedition were obliged to have recourse to their fire-arms before their assailants were driven back.

On the 6th of May, Saldé was reached, and the expedition was now well beyond hostile ground. A steamboat, the *Archimedes*, took on board Captain Gallieni and his companions, who reached St. Louis on the 12th May, and were welcomed by their friends there with many warm congratulations on their safe return.

The geographical results of Captain Gallieni's voyage were important, and the leader received, in recognition of his services, the medal of the Geographical Society of Paris, the gold medal of the Society of Bordeaux, and a diploma of honour from the French Geographical Congress of 1882.

CHAPTER VII.

DR. BARTH'S TRAVELS.

IN the year 1849 the British Government resolved to despatch an expedition to Central Africa, partly to explore the country, and partly to establish friendly relations with the chiefs and rulers of the various territories in the far interior. The command of the expedition was intrusted to Mr. Richardson, who had already distinguished himself in African travel. He was joined by Dr. Barth and Dr. Overweg, two German gentlemen who volunteered their services, on the Government expressing a wish that two foreigners should accompany the party. Dr. Barth was a professor in Germany who had attracted the notice of Lord Palmerston by his success in exploring the northern shores of Africa; while Dr. Overweg was a brave and energetic young fellow, thirty years of age.

The travellers started from Tripoli on the 29th March 1850. The journey was one of special interest, and there was a large gathering of friends to bid Mr. Richardson and his companions "God speed." Although the discoveries of previous travellers had shorn the adventure of much of its danger and mystery, sufficient peril remained to make parting friends feel that they might be looking on one another's faces for the last time. Such forebodings were sadly fulfilled, for before the small company reached Kúkawa, its leader, Mr. Richardson, fell ill and died. Dr. Barth, who was appointed to the command, and Dr. Overweg then separated for a time, exploring in different directions. When Barth returned to Kúkawa, he found his friend ill and exhausted. Within a week, Overweg too was gone, and Barth was left to explore alone the almost unknown regions of West Central Africa—to penetrate, if possible, the country as far as Timbuctoo, enter into treaty with the Sultan of Sokoto, and procure admission for European trade to this part of the Dark Continent. Some idea of the measure of success which he achieved may be gathered from the brief analysis of Barth's large volumes contained in the following pages.

On the death of his fellow-traveller, Mr. Overweg, Dr. Barth gave up his original plan of again trying his fortune in Kánem and on the north-east shores of the Tchad, and resolved to turn westwards and explore the countries on the middle course of the great river of the west, the I'sa or so-called Niger. He fixed upon Say, a town on the Niger somewhat south-east of Timbuctoo, as his first halting-place; but the main object of the expedition was to reach the town of Timbuctoo itself, a place attractive from the mystery by which it was surrounded.

It was on the 26th of November 1852 that Dr. Barth set out from Kúkawa, which had been his headquarters for more than twenty months. His little company consisted of an Arab sherif from Fez, who was going as far as Zinder, an interpreter from Jálo, five Mussulman freemen, and two liberated slaves, Dyrregu, a Houssa boy, and Abbega, a Marghi lad. Of Abbega Dr. Barth remarks: "He not unfrequently found some other object more interesting than my camels, which were intrusted to his care, and which in consequence he lost repeatedly."

The travellers had set out in the cool season of the African year, when, even in tropical Africa, in parts remote from the sea, that great equalizer of temperature, the nights are often positively cold. So to the delight of the travellers in once more finding themselves in the open country was added the enjoyment of a pleasant change of temperature, and also of scenery, as they exchanged the bleak and dreary hollows that lie between Káno and Kúkawa for rich fields waving with corn and fine crops of marákuwá and stubblefields of small millet. These pleasant changes, and the prospect of further novelty in the unknown regions of the far west, kept the travellers in the best of spirits.

By the 1st of December, Dr. Barth reached the Komádugu, the river-valley of Bornou. Recent rains had made the passage of this swampy network of channels and thick forests a most difficult task; but the travellers were encouraged by the sight of fine groups of trees and droves of guinea-fowl which now varied the scene. After visiting the site of Ghasréggomo, the old capital of Bornou, the travellers had to make a roundabout journey to reach the village of Zéngiri, where the river could be most easily forded. Having crossed the river, they entered the province of Manga, where some of the thievish natives robbed the Arab merchant in the most daring manner of his woollen blanket, dragging the poor fellow along in it until they forced him to let go. Passing through the walled town of Gesma, and places with such pleasant names as the "Queen of the Region of the Dúm Palm," and the "Sweetness of the World," they soon found themselves in the hilly district of Múniyó. There they were joined by parties of native traders, bearing their wares on their heads, as the British pedlar carries his on his back. The wooded hills, the many salt and fresh water lakes, the towns and villages, and cultivated land and pleasant pastures, with their herds of camels, horses, goats, sheep, and cattle, made the passage through Múniyó a very pleasant part of the journey. At one of the towns where they stopped to water the animals the wells were ten fathoms deep; and crowds of boys and girls were busy drawing water from two other larger wells on the north side of the place. The path was also frequented by numbers of people who were carrying the harvest into the town in nets made from the leaves of the dúm palm, and borne on the backs of oxen.

While passing through Múniyó, Dr. Barth, with two of his companions, visited a natron lake situated at the foot of a hill near a village called Magájiri. Dr. Barth writes: " When we had passed this village, which was full of natron (carbonate of soda), stored up partly in large piles into ' tákrufa ' or matting coverings, we obtained a view of the natron lake lying before us in the hollow at the foot of the rocky eminence, with its snow-white surface girt all round by a green border of luxuriant vegetation. This border of vegetation was formed by well-kept cotton grounds, which were just in flower, and by kitchen gardens, where derába was grown, the cultivated ground being broken by dúm bush and rank grass. Crossing this verdant and fertile strip, we reached the real natron lake, where we hesitated some time whether or not we should venture upon its surface; for the crust of natron was scarcely an inch thick, the whole of the ground underneath consisting of black boggy soil, from which the substance separates continually afresh." At the end of the rainy season the natron is obtained in larger pieces than at other times. "A large provision of natron, consisting of from twenty to twenty-five piles about ten yards in diameter and four in height, protected by a layer of reeds, was stored up at the northern end of the lake. The whole circumference of the basin was one mile and a half."

On Christmas day 1852, the travellers reached Zinder, a busy trading mart (Dr. Barth calls it "the gate of Soudan"), where they were to wait for new supplies. When these arrived, on the 20th of January, part of them was used to purchase from the natives such wares as red bernouses, turbans, looking-glasses, razors, chaplets, and gloves. Further on, at Kátsena, other purchases were made of cotton and silk goods made at Káno (the "Manchester of Africa") and Núpe, also of leather water-skins for covering luggage; "for," says Dr. Barth, "no place in the whole of Negroland is so famous for excellent leather and the art of tanning as Kátsena: and if I had taken a larger supply of these articles with me, it would have been very profitable; but of course these leather articles require a great deal of room." Among other purchases were two hundred and thirty-two black shawls for covering the face (these are the best presents for the Tawárek), seventy-five turkedis, and some of the tobacco of Kátsena, which is held in great estimation even in Timbuctoo. So provided, Dr. Barth knew he could pass safely through the countries on the middle course of the Niger, for these native manufactures are there everywhere a ready passport.

Leaving Kátsena, the travellers had to make a wide circuit on account of a hostile army known to be on the road. By keeping a good look-out, however, by marching at night, and sometimes by showing a bold front, or diving into the forests, they arrived, somewhat alarmed but uninjured, at Sokoto, the capital of the Fúlbe or Fellani, the most intelligent of all the African tribes. Though a small town, Sokoto can boast some five thousand inhabitants. It is a place of resort for numbers of the gray species of monkey. While there, Dr. Barth visited the house in which the traveller Clapperton died, and obtained some interesting information about the unfortunate captain's death. The market at Sokoto is thus described :—

"Even in the present reduced condition of the place, the market still presented a very interesting sight, the numerous groups of people, buyers as well as sellers, and the animals of various descriptions, being picturesquely scattered over the rocky slope. The market was tolerably well attended and well supplied, there being about thirty horses, three hundred head of cattle for slaughter, fifty oxen of burden, and a great quantity of leather articles, especially leather bags, cushions, and similar articles, the leather dressed and prepared here being very soft and beautiful. A good many slaves were exhibited, and fetched a higher price than might be supposed—a lad of very indifferent appearance being sold for thirty-three thousand shells. I myself bought a pony for thirty thousand shells. It being just about the time when the salt caravan visits these parts, dates also, which usually form a small addition to the principal merchandise of those traders of the desert, were to be had; and I filled a leather bag for some two thousand shells, in order to give a little more variety to my food on the long road which lay before me."

Much rice is grown near Sokoto, one whole valley forming an uninterrupted rice-field.

From Sokoto, the way of our travellers led to almost unknown regions, hitherto untrodden by European foot. As usual, the road lay through densely-peopled districts, where yams and corn-fields flourished. On some occasions Dr. Barth seems to have found the presents with which he had provided himself extremely useful. Such was the case with the sultan Aliyu, whom Dr. Barth visited to compliment the chief on his return from subduing some wretched little hamlets. "Although," he says, "I had made the chief a very respectable present on my first arrival, I thought it well to give greater impulse to his friendly disposition towards me by adding something also this time, presenting him with a cloth waistcoat and several smaller articles, besides a musical box, with the performance of which he was extremely pleased. But unfortunately when, anxious to impart his delight to his greatest friend and principal minister, he had called the latter

MARKET AT SOKOTO. Page 273.

to witness this wonder, the mysterious box, affected by the change of climate and the jolting of the long journey, was silent for a moment, and would not play. I may observe here that I think it better for travellers not to make such presents as musical boxes, which so easily get out of order.

"Having made a present to the ghaladima also, I thought it better, in order to make up for the deficiency of the musical box, to satisfy the musical taste of the sultan by making him a present of one of the harmonica which the Chevalier Bunsen (in consideration of the great effect which a missionary had produced with the aid of such an instrument on the inhabitants of the shores of the Nile) had procured for me; but I succeeded afterwards in repairing, in some measure, the musical box, which caused the good-natured chief inexpressible delight, so that he lost no time in writing for me a commendatory letter to his nephew, Khalilu, the chief of Gandu."

Passing through country which became more and more unsafe, Dr. Barth arrived at Gandu on the 17th of May. The Fúlbe prince, Khalilu, was well known for his intense dislike to Europeans and all Christians. An Arab who had gained influence at the sultan's court, however, managed a peaceful arrangement between the traveller and the chieftain, and no doubt the letter from the gratified owner of the musical box was not without effect; but it was only after some trouble and delay, and the sacrifice of many of his stores, that Dr. Barth was allowed, on the 4th of June, to proceed on his journey, which now promised to become of overwhelming interest as they neared the great African river, the object of their ambition.

The interest grew daily greater, though, owing to the heavy rains of that time of the year, their progress was but slow, and, owing to the unsafe state of the country, somewhat dangerous. One town had just been destroyed by the enemy, and all the inhabitants carried into slavery. "The aspect of the place was doleful and melancholy in the extreme, corresponding well with the dangerous situation in which we found ourselves; and whilst traversing the half-ruined village, which from a bustling little place had become the abode of death, I almost involuntarily snatched my gun and held it steadily in my hand. But life and death in these regions are closely allied; and we had scarcely left the ruined village behind us, when we were greeted by a most luxuriant rice-field, where the crops were already almost three feet high, and girt by the finest border of a nice variety of shady trees, overtopped by a number of tall deléb palms, the golden fruit of which, half ripe, was starting forth from under the feathery foliage. But our attention was soon diverted from the enjoyment of this scenery to a point of greater interest to ourselves. We here observed a solitary individual, in spite of the unsafe state of the country, sitting quietly at the foot of one of the palm trees, and seemingly enjoying its fruit. Now, coupling the present state of the country with the news we had just received, we could not help greatly suspecting this man to be a spy, posted here by the enemy in order to give them information of the passers-by; and I had the greatest difficulty in preventing my Arab, who, when there was no danger for himself, always mustered a great amount of courage, from shooting this suspicious-looking character."

Proceeding further through this rich but unsafe district, the travellers, to their great delight, met a solitary and courageous pilgrim—a Jolof, from the shores of the Atlantic—carrying his little luggage on his head, and seemingly well prepared to defend it with his double-barrelled gun which he carried on his shoulder, and a short sword hanging at his side, while his shirt was tossed gallantly up and tied over his shoulder behind the neck. "In my joy at the sight of this enterprising native traveller," says Dr. Barth, "I could not forbear making him a small present, in order to assist him in his arduous undertaking."

At the strong walled town of Kóla, which commands the whole passage of the great valley of Kebbi, the company made a short halt to insure peace with the powerful governor of the place, who was said to command as many as seventy musketeers. Having made him a small present, they were hospitably received both by the governor and his sister, the latter showing her favour by the gift of a goose—a most welcome present to a European somewhat tired of the usual African fare.

At the border of the valley were some fine pasture grounds, where some horses were grazing; but the herbage was full of small venomous snakes, which repeatedly crossed the path of the travellers in large numbers.

But soon they left the cultivated grounds and entered a dense forest, which had a very pleasant appearance, all the trees being in blossom, and spreading a delightful fragrance around. There, too, they were agreeably surprised to come upon two extensive ponds, which supplied them with delicious water (though on their return journey, in August 1854, they were equally but disagreeably surprised to find the water of these same ponds had so changed as to almost poison the whole company). The travellers pitched their tent in the midst of the forest, Dr. Barth greatly enjoying the open encampment again, after the dirty huts in which he had lately been obliged to live. However, they had to enjoy this wild encampment longer than they wished, as one of the camels was lost in the desert, and must be found before they could proceed. This experience gained for Dr. Barth the fame among the people of the neighbourhood of being the only man who had spent a day in the unsafe wilderness.

Pushing on up the fertile though wretched valley of the Fógha, with its numerous salt-lakes, its fields of yams and tobacco, and herds of elephants, through dense forests and fields where fresh crops were just shooting up, through swampy ground covered with rank grass, Dr. Barth and his companions reached Songhay, a farming village, full of corn-stacks, and inhabited by serfs. All the huts in these Songhay villages consist merely of reeds; and while they are less solid than the clay dwellings of the Kebbi, they are better ventilated and have a less offensive smell. Here they found a jovial old farmer, who not only supplied the travellers with milk and corn, but even made Dr. Barth the present of a sheep.

A period of great drought now set in, and owing to the heat and the weak condition of his camels, Dr. Barth had to be content with short marches through parched and uncultivated ground, then for a short distance through country partly laid out in fields, partly covered with underwood, until at length they reached a village where they could quarter, though not until they had used force to obtain a hut for their use—the head man of the village being too lazy, or too obstinate, to leave his cool shed in the heat of the day.

"We were now," Dr. Barth writes, "close to the

Niger; and I was justified in indulging in the hope that I might the next day behold with my own eyes that great river of Western Africa, which has caused such intense curiosity in Europe, and the upper part of the large eastern branch of which I had myself discovered."

These expectations were soon fulfilled, for next day, Monday, June 20th (our Queen's accession day), Dr. Barth sighted the Niger.

"Next morning," he writes, "at an early hour, I set out; and after a march of a little less than two hours, through a rocky wilderness covered with dense bushes, I obtained the first sight of the river; and in less than an hour more, during which I was in constant sight of this noble spectacle, I reached the place of embarkation opposite the town of Say.

"In a noble, unbroken stream, though here, where it has become contracted, only about seven hundred yards broad, hemmed in on this side by a rocky bank of from twenty to thirty feet in elevation, the great river of Western Africa (whose name under all its many forms means nothing but 'the river,' and which therefore may well continue to be called the Niger) was gliding along in a north-easterly and south-westerly direction, with a moderate current of about three miles an hour. On the flatter shore opposite, a large town was spreading out, the low ramparts and huts of which were picturesquely over-

SONGHAY VILLAGE.

Page 281.

topped by numbers of slender dúm palms. This was the river-town or 'ford,'—the name Say meaning, in this eastern dialect, 'the river.' The banks at present were not high; but the river, as it rises, approaches the very border of the rocky slope."

While waiting for the boats which were to carry them across the river, the travellers had plenty of leisure for observing the river scenery, and the passengers crossing in the smaller boats, Fúlbe and Songhay natives, with asses and pack-oxen. At length the boats, or rather canoes, which were to carry Dr. Barth's company and their effects across, made their appearance. "They were of good size, about forty feet in length, and from four to five feet in width in the middle, consisting of two trunks of trees hollowed out and sewn together in the middle. These boats are chiefly used for carrying corn from Sínder, a town higher up the river, to Say; and they had been expressly sent for by the 'king of the waters,' as the inspector of the harbour is called. The largest of them was able to carry three of my camels; and the water was kept out much better than I had ever yet found to be the case with the native craft of the inhabitants of Negroland.

"My camels, horses, people, and luggage having crossed over without accident, I myself followed about one o'clock in the afternoon, filled with delight when floating on the waters of this celebrated stream, the exploration of which had cost the sacrifice of so many noble lives."

To Dr. Barth the sight of the river was of the more importance, because he was so soon again to leave it and proceed by land to Timbuctoo—that being the only route so far as he then knew; and he had only a faint hope of revisiting the river between Timbuctoo and Say. In doubt of ever being able to reach the western coast, our traveller thought it more interesting to survey the course of the Niger between the point already explored by Mungo Park and the lower portion known through the accounts of the Landers, than to cross the whole of Central Africa.

Having presented himself at the governor's house, Dr. Barth soon obtained quarters, though they were not at all to his taste, being small and narrow. The town, in its very low position, is not refreshed by a single current of air, and has a very oppressive atmosphere. The huts, too, seemed made rather for women than for men, the women's apartment occupying the greater part of each. The bedstead, made of the branches of trees, was enclosed in a separate chamber of mats, thus leaving only a very small entrance, and blocking up the inside of the dwelling. Dr. Barth's first task was to demolish one of these small matting bed-rooms in order to obtain some ventilation. At length, having made himself somewhat comfortable, he began to long for some refreshment, having been exposed to the sun during the hottest part of the day. The governor, however, sent only stores of rice and millet, which had to be husked and cooked before the travellers could satisfy their hunger. The town was suffering from want of rain, and the air of the valley, always oppressive, became almost suffocating.

Next morning Dr. Barth rode round the town of Say, which he describes as of quadrangular shape, with a low rampart of earth on three of its sides, the fourth, looking towards the river, being unprotected. Though pretty large, the town is but thinly inhabited, the dwellings, all except the governor's, consisting of matting and reeds, lying scattered about like so many separate hamlets. It is divided by a wide valley running from north to south, surrounded by dúm palms, which are almost the only trees either inside or outside the town. At the end of the rainy season this valley becomes filled with water, stopping the business and adding to the unhealthiness of the town. "There can be no doubt," Dr. Barth thinks, "that in seasons when the river reaches an unusual height the whole town is under water, the inhabitants being obliged to seek safety beyond the borders of the valley."

In the eastern part of the town, not far from the river, a market is held every day, which, poor as it is, is of some importance; and hence the town has a great name as a market-place among the inhabitants of Western Soudan, many of whom here supply their want of native manufactures, especially of common clothing for both men and women, as the art of weaving and dyeing is there greatly neglected, and very little cotton is grown. But the place was most miserably supplied with provisions, there being no store of grain whatever. Everything necessary was brought day by day from the town called Sínder, about eighty miles higher up the river. To Dr. Barth's great surprise, not a grain of rice is grown here, though the soil, being often under water, is particularly suited for rice-growing. Everything at Say was very dear, especially butter, which was scarcely to be procured at all. The money used in the market consisted of shells. The high prices depended on the state of feeling between Say and Haúsa, and it so chanced that at the time of Dr. Barth's visit that was not of the most peaceful kind.

"For the English, or Europeans in general, Say is," writes Dr. Barth, "the most important place in all this tract of the river, if only they succeed in crossing the rapids above Rabba, and especially between Busa and Yauri, and reach this fine open sheet of water, the great highroad of Western Central Africa."

Being now about to enter a new country, where the natives spoke a language which none of the company understood, and not being able to give much time to its study, Dr. Barth was very anxious to obtain the services of a native of the country, or to liberate a Songhay slave; but he did not succeed at the time, and so did not feel so much at home in the countries through which he now had to pass.

As he left the great river behind, Dr. Barth's thoughts turned with intense interest to the new and unexplored region before him. However, on the very first day of their march (June 24th) the travellers had a sufficient specimen of what awaited them during the rainy season. They had scarcely left the low island behind on which the town of Say, that hot-bed of fever, is situated, and ascended the steep rocky bank which borders the west side of the river, when a dark array of thunder-clouds came, as it were, marching on them from the south-east, and a terrible thunderstorm suddenly broke out, beginning with a most fearful sand-wind, which wrapped the whole district in the darkness of night, and made progress for a moment quite impossible. After a while it was followed by a violent rain, which relieved the sand-storm, but lasted for nearly three hours, filling the path with water to the depth of several inches, and soaking the unfortunate explorers through to the skin, making the rest of their march very uncomfortable. They at last found shelter in a farming hamlet, where the people were busily employed in sowing, the plentiful rain, which was the first of the season, having rendered the fields fit for cultivation. The proprietor, a cheerful and wealthy old man, lodged the company comfortably in two round huts near a sheep-pen in front of his dwelling. While his people were drying themselves and their luggage, Dr. Barth roved about a little, watching the women washing their clothes in pools of stagnant water and the slaves busy working in the fields.

Their way at first lay through hilly country, sometimes varied by pleasant vales or glens, though in general they were treeless and thinly inhabited. After a short march they reached the highest point, from which they could view an extensive wilderness, with only a few cultivated spots hidden in the forest. Passing through some picturesque but not very fertile regions, they arrived at the town of Champagore, a town enclosed by hills, and remarkable for its magazines of corn, which consist of towers or square buildings, raised a few feet above the ground, in order to protect them from the ants. They have no opening at the bottom, but only a kind of window near the top, through which the corn is taken in and out; and on the whole they are not unlike the dove-cots of Egypt. These magazines, one or two of which are to be seen in every courtyard, far surpass in their appearance the dwellings themselves, which are nearly all low huts, enclosed by a frail fence made of the stalks of the native corn.

Before leaving this place Dr. Barth visited the chief. The portal of the residence was very stately; but the spacious courtyard inside, which was enclosed by a low clay wall, full of rubbish, and poor, mean-looking huts, did not correspond with the stately entrance. However, the dwelling itself, although simple, was not mean, and, besides two spacious clay halls, included some very airy and cool corridors built entirely of wood. Having been first received in one of the clay halls by the chief, a very pleasant-looking man of middle height, about seventy years of age, in a simple light-blue tobe, with a white shawl wound round his face, Dr. Barth was conducted afterwards to one of the corridors for a more private audience, and there delivered his present—a red cap, half a piece of muslin, and other smaller articles.

This old chief, Galaijo, had received a large though not very fertile district from the chief of Gandu; and so the travellers found here a small court and a people bearing no resemblance whatever to those around them, having faithfully preserved the manners and institutions of their native country. While all the neighbouring natives are rather a slender race of men, with fine, sharply-cut features, who make it a rule to dress in white colours, here were found people quite the reverse—a set of sturdy men, with round open countenances, and long black curly hair, all clad alike in light-blue tobes, and nearly all armed with muskets.

Three of Galaijo's servants, all armed with muskets, attached themselves to the company of travellers; and in case of any attack on the road, were supplied with ball cartridges, for the way now lay through an unsafe wilderness. A few miles from their starting-point they passed some strange smelting-furnaces, about six feet high, and measuring a foot and a half across the base. The native smelting is a very simple process. On the ironstone is placed a large quantity of wood-ashes. When the metal begins to melt, it is received, by three channels at the bottom of the furnace, into a little trough or basin. Soon after this they came upon numerous footprints of the elephant, and traces of the rhinoceros. Monkey-bread trees were here seen in great abundance.

One day their progress was stopped by the sudden bend of a river, about seventy yards wide, which they were to cross merely on bundles of reeds that they were themselves to tie together. At length, after much bargaining, some natives agreed to assist the travellers in crossing. While the large bundles of the frail ferry were being tied together, the head man of the village and many of the natives watched the operation from the high banks. The men formed interesting groups, with their short shirts and wide trowsers of light blue, and their short pipes in their mouths, for they smoked incessantly. Their features, though effeminate, were full of expression, their hair plaited in long tresses and hanging over their cheeks, sometimes even to their shoulders. The women were short of stature and unshapely, and had their necks and ears richly ornamented with strings of beads, but none of them wore the nose-ring. The men were clever swimmers, and carried the small luggage across the river in calabashes; but it took two hours to convey the whole party and their luggage safely to the other side.

Continuing their march through the forest, they found numerous footprints of the elephant and the buffalo, and ere long fell in with a large herd of the latter cropping the luxuriant grass of the pasture grounds. In the province of Yagha, through which they were now passing, they found the natives busily occupied, some in weaving on sticks hung from the roof, others in basket-making and leather-work. At one of these huts Dr. Barth put up for a night, and writes of it thus:—

"The clay being excellently polished, and the hut of recent construction, left a very pleasant impression; but, as is often the case in human life, all this finery covered nothing but misery, and I discovered the next day, to my utter amazement, that this beautiful hut was one entire nest of ants, which had in one day made great havoc with the whole of my luggage."

As he passed on, more serious dangers threatened our brave explorer, from the hatred of the natives against all Christians, or, as they called them, infidels, and their suspicions of Dr. Barth. On one occasion, indeed, he only narrowly escaped death by adopting the advice of an Arab, and representing himself as an officer carrying books to the sheik. The plan succeeded; for the large company of furious half-naked men, brandishing their weapons over their heads in a most threatening manner, "all of a sudden dropped their spears and thronged round me," Dr. Barth says, "requesting me to give them my blessing; and the circumstances under which I was placed obliged me to comply with this slight request, although it was by no means a pleasant matter to lay my hands on all those dirty heads."

These same people proved in the end most useful. Having received his blessing, they conducted the traveller to a place where they declared the water to be fordable. The ground, however, even here proved boggy, and the luggage had to be carried across by the people, the camels nearly sticking in the bog, even though unloaded; while Dr. Barth, being persuaded by the natives that his dignity in presence of the native travellers absolutely required him to remain on horseback, fell under his horse in the middle of the swamp. His journals got wet through, and they had the greatest difficulty in extricating the poor horse from the bog.

On his passage through the district of Aribinda

(that is, "the place beyond or south of the water"), Dr. Barth's luggage suffered somewhat from the many water-courses which he had to cross, and the greed of the Arabs. One governor, to whom he had already made several presents, somewhat astonished our traveller when he was setting out by begging the very tobe which he then was wearing!

In one village of industrious natives Dr. Barth found some of his English goods very acceptable, especially some English darning-needles, which fetched a very high price, though the small common needles were regarded with the utmost contempt.

One of the most dangerous stages of the journey was that which lay through the country of the Tawárek, for there the crafty Arab companion of Dr. Barth could take full advantage of the European's dangerous situation. "On the one hand," says Dr. Barth, "it had become necessary to represent me to these simple people as a great sherif, and thus to excite their hospitable feelings, while at the same time he instigated me to reward their treatment in a generous manner, but nevertheless sold my presents to them as his own property! It required a great deal of patience on my part to bear up against the numerous delays in this part of our journey, and to endure the many tricks played upon me by the treachery of my companion, in order to prevent at least his proceeding to open violence."

At one place, on the departure of Dr. Barth, the whole population, both men and women, turned out to receive his blessing. "Among the women," Dr. Barth writes, "I discovered a few pretty young girls, especially one whose beauty was enhanced by her extreme shyness in approaching me; but their dress was very poor indeed, consisting of coarse cotton stuff, which was wrapped round the body and brought down over the head." All the boys of the same place under twelve years of age had the left side of their head entirely shaven, while from the crop on the right side a long curl hung down.

At another place they had a sign that they were approaching Timbuctoo, in the anxiety of the people to taste tea, which they called the water of Simsim, from the celebrated well of that name in Mecca. At another encampment farther on, the eagerness of the women to obtain tobacco was very remarkable, and they pestered the travellers during great part of the night by their demands for the luxury.

On the 27th of August the explorers set out on their last journey by land, in order to reach the place where they were to embark on the river. At the town of Sarayamo they found a great many people collected to receive them; and after firing a salute with their pistols, they obtained, after some search, quarters large enough to admit the luggage.

No sooner was the explorer settled than he was

visited by a number of the more important natives, one of whom thought it strange that the so-called Syrian chief could not say his prayers with him in the courtyard. To allay the suspicions as to his religion, Dr. Barth on one occasion felt himself obliged to repeat the opening prayer of the Koran, concluding, to the great amusement and delight of his hearers, with the Arabic words meaning, "God may give water;" which have become quite a common complimentary phrase—perhaps like our "Good-bye"—few people thinking of its original meaning. It so happened that on the following night a heavy thunderstorm came on, bringing rain. Next day the inhabitants returned to beg a repetition of the stranger's performance. On the other hand, however, a blessing administered along with a strong emetic to the governor, who was setting out for the capital, turned out less successful; for though the governor was well received in the capital, he was greatly shocked to learn that his blessing was that of a Christian.

At the large island of Kora, where the Futta branch of the Niger joins the main stream, the travellers were able to embark again on the Niger. In the neighbourhood through which they had just passed, the great river forms such a network of creeks, backwaters, and channels, as to spread over the whole country. Dr. Barth had hired a large boat from Timbuctoo for the exclusive use of his party, and great was his satisfaction when, on the 1st of September, he found himself floating on the backwater which was to carry him to the harbour of Timbuctoo. The boats were pushed along by poles, the water being often blocked by reeds and other growth, so that they seemed to be sailing over a grassy plain. The abundant fish kept them well supplied with fresh food; and as they proceeded, great lizards, called zangways, basked at night, while still further down alligators and hippopotami were seen. Where the Futta joined the Niger stood a solitary group of trees, "which appeared," says Barth, "to form the usual nightly place of resort for all the water-fowl of the neighbourhood, the trunks as well as the branches of the trees showing traces of these visitors."

At this point they left the shore, and entered the middle of the magnificent Niger river, called here the I'sa or Mayo Balleo. At this spot, about a mile across, the magnitude and solemn magnificence of the place under the rising moon were enhanced by the summer-lightning at times breaking through the evening sky; and Barth says his servants were inspired with real awe and almost fright, "while we were squatting on the shelving roof of our frail boat, and looked with searching eyes along the immense expanse of the river in a north-easterly direction, where the object of our journey was said to lie."

The excitement of the day, or the previous night's wetting, brought a severe attack of fever on Barth when they lay-to at the town of Koiretago; but in order to guard his luggage, he refused to go on shore and sleep on the fine sandy beach, but remained on board the frail boat.

From this point, Barth followed close upon the track of the unfortunate traveller Major Laing, who had been assassinated two years before on his desperate journey from Timbuctoo.

The river Niger was, where Barth crossed it, about three-quarters of a mile broad, but in the rainy season it lays the whole country to a great distance under water. Yet, except for a few fishing-boats, the grand river was tenantless. At one of the villages on this part of the river Barth received the unwelcome news that the sheik, El Bakay, on whose noble and trustworthy character he had placed his hopes of success, was away in Gundam.

At Kabara, where a numerous fleet of good-sized boats was lying, Barth was visited by a party of armed men, horse and foot, from Timbuctoo, most of them clad in light-blue tobes, tightly girt round the waist with a shawl, and short breeches, their heads covered with a pointed straw hat. As they were busy in protecting their cattle from the Tawárek, they did not molest our traveller, except by their rude curiosity.

Meanwhile a messenger had been despatched to Timbuctoo to obtain protection for our traveller, and in the evening Sheik El Bakay's brother arrived with his followers. Under the escort and protection of this chieftain, Barth proceeded the next day, September 7th, to Timbuctoo.

The way at first lay through a desert tract, thickly lined with thorny bushes and stunted trees, infested by the Tawárek. This short road between the harbour and the town is so unsafe that it bears the remarkable name, Ur-immándes ("he does not hear"), because the cry of the unfortunate victim cannot be heard from either side.

As they approached the town, the travellers were met by a body of people who had come out to bid the stranger welcome. "This was," says Dr. Barth, "a very important moment, as, if they had felt the slightest suspicion with regard to my character, they might easily have prevented my entering the town at all, and thus even endangered my life.

"I therefore took the hint of Alawate, who recommended me to make a start in advance and anticipate the salute of these people who had come to meet us; and putting my horse to a gallop, and gun in hand, I galloped up to meet them, when I was received with many salaams. But a circumstance occurred which might have proved fatal not only to my enterprise, but even to my own personal safety, as there was a man

TIMBUCTOO.

Page 302.

among the group who addressed me in Turkish, which I had almost entirely forgotten, so that I could with difficulty make a suitable answer to his compliment; but avoiding further indiscreet questions, I pushed on in order to get under safe cover.

"Having then traversed the rubbish which has accumulated round the ruined clay wall of the town, and left on one side a row of dirty reed huts, which encompass the whole of the place, we entered the narrow streets and lanes, which scarcely allowed two horses to proceed abreast. But I was not a little surprised at the populous and wealthy character which this quarter of the town exhibited, many of the houses rising to the height of two stories. Followed by a numerous troop of people, we passed the house of the sheik, El Bakay, where I was desired to fire a pistol; but as I had all my arms loaded with ball, I prudently declined to do so, and left it to one of my people to do honour to the house of our host. We thus reached the house on the other side of the street which was destined for my residence, and I was glad when I found myself safely in my new quarters."

In Timbuctoo, the city of his hopes, unlooked-for trials awaited the brave traveller, and for long his life was endangered. The same Arab who had suggested that Dr. Barth should pass as a Mohammedan proved treacherous, and no sooner was it known that he was an infidel, as they called a Christian, than a party arose demanding either his expulsion or his death. Probably some heavy bribes might have soon quieted the clamour, but such means do not seem to have been tried; and so their seven months' residence in the city was a dangerous and exciting time for Barth and his party.

Although it had been arranged that during the absence of the sheik, El Bakay, whose special guest Barth was to be, no one should be allowed to see him, still numbers of inquisitive people gained access to his house, to the annoyance of the traveller, who was seriously ill. On the second day his health began to improve, however, and he received the visits of several respectable people.

We cannot sufficiently admire the courage and self-reliance, the prudence and patience and industrious observation of our traveller at this trying time in Timbuctoo. For a time he was a prisoner in all but name. He writes thus:—

"I was not allowed to stir about, but was confined within the walls of my house. In order to obviate the effect of this want of exercise as much as possible, to enjoy fresh air, and at the same time to become familiar with the principal features of the town, through which I was not allowed to move about at pleasure, I ascended as often as possible the terrace of my house. This afforded an excellent view over the northern quarter of the town. The style of the buildings was various. I could see clay houses of different characters, some low and unseemly, others rising with a second story in front to greater elevation, the whole being interrupted by a few round huts of matting. The streets being very narrow, only little was to be seen of the intercourse carried on in them, with the exception of the small market in the northern quarter, which was exposed to view on account of its situation on the slope of the sand-hills which, in course of time, have accumulated round the mosque.

"But while the terrace of my house seemed to make me well acquainted with the character of the town, it had also the disadvantage of exposing me fully to the gaze of the passers-by, so that I could only slowly, and with many interruptions, succeed in making a sketch of the scene thus offered to my view."

Our traveller made use of his leisure time during his imprisonment to send articles into the market, he himself purchasing some calico. In these peaceful occupations he was, however, disturbed by a rumour that his enemies were coming to attack him in his house. Barth suspecting his pretended friends to be at the bottom of the rumour, treated it with contempt. At the same time he improved his position in the town, at least with the more intelligent inhabitants, by a skilful discussion in favour of Christianity as opposed to Mohammedanism.

On the 13th of September our traveller received a friendly letter from El Bakay, to which he at once replied; and on the 26th the sheik himself arrived in Timbuctoo. Barth, being still unwell, had to put off receiving the sheik's visit until the following day, when they had a long conversation, chiefly concerning the unfortunate African traveller Major Laing, whose great bodily strength and noble and chivalrous character the sheik could not sufficiently admire. Soon after the interview, Barth sent the sheik a handsome present, consisting of three bernouses, a Turkey carpet, four tobes, twenty Spanish dollars in silver, three black shawls, and other articles, the whole amounting to the value of about £30. In thanking Barth for his liberality, the sheik stated that he desired no more of the traveller at present; but begged that on his safe return home Barth should not forget him, but request Her Majesty's Government to send him some good fire-arms and some Arabic books. This Barth willingly pledged himself to do.

On one occasion the sheik made Barth fire off his six-barrelled pistol in front of the residence, before a numerous company of people. This caused great excitement and astonishment among the people, and exercised a great influence upon Barth's future safety, as it made them believe he had arms all over his person, and could fire as many times as he liked.

On the 1st of October a body of armed men

ENCAMPMENT OF SHEIK EL BAKAY. *Page 306.*

arrived from the residence of the sheik to whose nominal sway the town of Timbuctoo and the whole province had been subjected for many years. They brought with them an order to expel the stranger out of the town. This roused the spirit of El Bakay, who resolved to show that he was able to protect the traveller, whom he now removed for a short time to his camp without the town. This change was agreeable to Barth. He had more liberty and exercise, better air, and more varied scenery; but his pleasure was marred by plots and intrigues. On the 13th he returned to Timbuctoo; and although the city was much disturbed by warfare between the different tribes, he was able to explore the place more carefully. The stately appearance of Timbuctoo seems to have made a deep impression on the traveller's mind.

The dangers of Dr. Barth's position were increasing daily, and soon he was again removed to the encampment of El Bakay. In vain he urged his protector to provide the means of escape. His enemies were not now confined to one small party;—their name was legion. Every week fresh parties kept arriving with orders to seize the stranger, dead or alive. One of these parties actually attacked the camp, but was driven back by the brave traveller and his faithful protectors. In fact, as Barth says, his mere presence in the city or its neighbourhood seemed to have upset the daily life of the whole community. To add to the traveller's misery, he was the constant victim of fever, for Timbuctoo is by no means a healthy place.

At last a fortunate chance turned the tide of persecution. On the 19th of December the chief of the Berabish, who had arrived with a large body of armed followers to take our traveller's life, fell suddenly sick and died.

"His death," says Dr. Barth, "made an extraordinary impression upon the people, as it was a well-known fact that it was his father who had killed Major Laing, the former Christian who had visited this place; and the more so, as it was generally believed that I was Major Laing's son.

"The people could not but think that there was some supernatural connection between the death of this man, at this place and at this period, and the murderous deed perpetrated by his father; and, on the whole, I cannot but think that this event exercised a salutary influence upon my final safety. The followers of the chief of the Berabish were so frightened, that they came in great procession to the sheik El Bakay to beg his pardon for their neglect, and to obtain his blessing; "nay, the old man himself," Barth writes, "a short time afterwards sent word that he would in no way interfere with my departure, but wished nothing better than that I might reach home in safety."

The river was at this time rising rapidly, and soon

filled the valleys of this sandy region. On Christmas day, 1853, the water entered the wells round the southern part of the town—an event which happens only about every third year. At the end of January the inundation of the Niger reached its height. Soon boats began to arrive from other towns, bringing supplies of corn, so that provisions at Timbuctoo became much cheaper.

Of Timbuctoo as a trading town Dr. Barth says: "Almost the whole life of the city is based on foreign commerce, for the splendid river enables the inhabitants to supply all their wants from without. Native corn is not raised here in sufficient quantities to feed even a very small proportion of the population.

"The only manufactures of the city, as far as fell under my observation, are confined to the art of the blacksmith and to a little leather-work. Some of these articles, such as provision or luggage bags, cushions, small leather pouches for tobacco, and gun-cloths, especially the leather bags, are very neat; but even these are mostly manufactured at Tawárek, and especially by females, so that the industry of the city is hardly of any account."

Not much dyeing or weaving is done in Timbuctoo, clothing being chiefly imported from other places. Some of the natives, however, are very skilful in adorning their clothing with a fine stitching of silk; and those of some of the neighbouring districts produce excellent woollen blankets and carpets of various colours, which are in great demand among the natives.

Many articles used in Timbuctoo Dr. Barth found to be of English manufacture, brought either through Morocco or by way of Sivera, where there are many European merchants. All the cutlery used in Timbuctoo is of English workmanship; all the calico Barth saw bore the name of one and the same Manchester firm, printed in Arabic letters. Tea was largely bought by the Arabs, though still too dear for the natives. Tobacco, red cloth, sashes, and looking-glasses seemed in great demand.

Almost the only things sent out from Timbuctoo at the time of Dr. Barth's visit seemed to be gold, some gum and wax, a little ivory, and occasionally a few slaves. The place seemed to him to offer a great field for European trade, were it not for the difficulties in the way of free intercourse with Europeans. The position of the town, at the edge of the desert and on the border of various tribes, seemed to make a strong government very difficult, almost impossible; while its distance from the west coast or the mouth of the Niger made it inaccessible. Yet, on the other hand, the great facilities of the noble river, and the security by a mountain chain and a tract of frightful desert from all danger of French attack from Algeria or Senegal, and the former friendly feelings of the natives towards the English, seemed to point to a sure way for English pioneers.

After many delays on account of the illness of Dr. Barth, and other reasons, and one or two false starts, a final and real start from Timbuctoo was made on the 18th of May. It must have been with no small delight that our traveller found himself at last free for ever from the turbulent Fúlbe and Tawárek and their swampy regions. He found the country gradually improved. The route lay partly along the banks of the magnificent river, on beautiful sandy beaches, at times shut in by downs, richly clad with dúm palms and other trees. The prevalence of swamps, however, forced the travellers occasionally to a distance from the river; but even there the country was enlivened by grassy creeks, with groves and villages, and herds of cattle, sheep, and goats.

Without any serious perils our traveller reached Gogo, the ancient capital of a strong and mighty empire. "Cheered at having reached this spot," writes Dr. Barth, "I passed a tranquil night, and rising early in the morning, lay down outside my tent, quietly enjoying the prospect over this once busy locality, which, according to many writers, was once the most splendid city of Negroland, though it is now the desolate abode of a small and miserable population. Just opposite to my tent was a ruined massive tower, the last remains of the principal mosque of the capital, the sepulchre of the great conqueror Mohammed."

Except this tower, however, all that remained of the once great city of Negroland was some three to four hundred huts, in separate groups, and surrounded by heaps of rubbish. Here an old man offered to conduct our traveller to a place of interest, and led him through the rubbish to a long narrow clay building; but the master of the house refused them admittance. Dr. Barth seems to think this may have been the burial-place of Mungo Park.

To the south of this old capital of Negroland the country improved greatly, and on July 9th Barth, bidding farewell to his kind old friend El Bakay, who had escorted him thus far, crossed the river some ten miles below Gogo. From this place to Say, where he had first crossed the river, a distance of more than two hundred and fifty miles, was traversed in safety, except for an alarming adventure with some mounted natives, who mistook his party for a hostile army, and were about to attack them. In the half-civilized regions through which the return journey lay, there was the same trouble with greedy rulers, the same annoyances from thievish, hostile natives, the same trials of rains, swamps, and fevers, that had marked the outward journey. More than once, too, their supplies gave out, and threatened them with starvation. At the town of Sokoto a pleasant surprise awaited them in the shape of news that Mr. Vogel and a party of English travellers sent out by Government had arrived in Kúkawa.

Dr. Barth thus describes his meeting with Mr. Vogel: "Having rejoined my camels, I set out without delay through the forest, taking the lead with my head servant; but I had scarcely proceeded three miles when I saw advancing towards me a person of strange aspect—a young man of very fair complexion, dressed in a tobe like the one I wore myself, and with a white turban wound thickly round his head. He was accompanied by two or three blacks, likewise on horseback. One of them I recognized as my servant Madi, whom, on setting out from Kúkawa, I had left in the house as a guardian. As soon as he saw me he told the young man that I was Abd el Kérim; in consequence of which Mr. Vogel (for he it was) rushed forward, and, taken by surprise as both of us were, we gave each other a hearty reception from horseback. As for myself, I had not had the remotest expectation of meeting him; and he, on his part, had only a short time before received the intelligence of my safe return from the west. Not having the slightest notion that I was alive, and judging from its Arab address that the letter which I forwarded to him from Kanó was a letter from some Arab, he had put it by without opening it, waiting till he might meet with a person who should be able to read it.

"In the midst of this inhospitable forest we dismounted and sat down together on the ground; and my camels having arrived, I took out my small bag of provisions, and had some coffee boiled, so that we were quite at home. It was with great amazement that I heard from my young friend that there were no supplies in Kúkawa; that what he had brought with him had been spent; and that the usurper, Abd e' Rahmán, had treated him very badly, having even taken possession of the property which I had left in Zinder."

Soon the rest of the caravan came up, and were amazed to find their leader quietly conversing with a friend in the midst of the forest, while the whole district was infested by hostile men.

After arranging to meet in Kúkawa before the end of the month, the two friends separated, Mr. Vogel going on to Zinder, Dr. Barth hastening to overtake his people.

On reaching safely the town of Kúkawa, from which place he had first commenced his journeys of exploration into Negroland, it might seem as if our traveller had at last overcome all his difficulties, and should be able to enjoy a short rest before setting out on the last stage of his homeward journey. But such was not the case, and he had to pass four rather unpleasant months in the town. Being in want of money, and finding that a great part of Mr. Vogel's stores had been abstracted, Dr. Barth explained these matters to the sheik, to whom he first made a present of about £8 in money. By so doing he incurred the dislike of one of the most influential courtiers, whose servant, or more probably himself, had obtained the greater share of the plunder. Another disagreeable circumstance was the unfriendly relation between Mr. Vogel and Corporal Church, one of his sappers, which Dr. Barth did his best to improve.

More pleasant occupation was found in looking over the books Mr. Vogel had brought with him, and also re-reading a packet of letters, some dated as far back as December 1851, found in a box which had been plundered. Partly in fulfilment of a vow he had made, and partly to make the natives more friendly towards him, Dr. Barth made a present to the inhabitants of the capital on Christmas day of fourteen oxen, not forgetting either rich or poor, blind or maimed, nor even the Arab strangers.

On the 29th of December Mr. Vogel returned to Kúkawa, and Dr. Barth and the brave enterprising young traveller spent twenty days together very pleasantly, the latter quickly adapting himself to the strange new life. In his youthful enthusiasm, however, Mr. Vogel seems sometimes to have made the mistake of expecting that his companions, recently arrived from Europe, perhaps with less elevated ideas of their mission, should, like himself, give up all their pretensions to comfort. Thus quarrels arose, and hindered the work of the party sent out by Government. The more experienced and the young traveller, however, passed their time very pleasantly, exchanging opinions about the countries both had already traversed, and making plans for Mr. Vogel's future course, Dr. Barth giving his young friend much information, and the care of clearing up several undecided points.

"Thus," he writes, "we began cheerfully the year 1855, in which I was to return to Europe from my long career of hardships and privations, and in which my young friend was to endeavour to complete my discoveries and researches.

"Meanwhile some interesting excursions to the shores of the Tchad formed a pleasant interruption in our course of studies and scientific communication; and these little trips were especially interesting on account of the extraordinary manner in which the shores of the lake had been changed since I last saw them."

There were two subjects which caused Dr. Barth anxiety about the future of the enterprising young explorer Mr. Vogel;—the first, his want of experience, for he was still a young man, and fresh from Europe; the other was his weakness of digestion, which made it impossible for him to eat meat of any kind. The very sight of a dish of meat made him sick.

Having assisted Mr. Vogel with all his preparations,

and foreseeing trouble with the transporting of his rather heavy and unusual luggage, the older traveller escorted his young friend out of the town on the 20th of January, bearing him company in the following day's march, and leaving him with the best of wishes. Corporal Macguire went on with Mr. Vogel, but it was thought best for Corporal Church to return to Europe with Dr. Barth—perhaps because of the frequent disagreements between him and his young commanding officer.

This was the last Dr. Barth saw of the brave young explorer, who set out so cheerfully and hopefully. It is supposed that he was afterwards murdered, while Macguire probably shared a similar fate, on his way home, at the well of Bedwáram.

Barth meanwhile returned to Kúkawa, feeling rather desolate and lonely. The cold to which he had been exposed on the previous night brought on a violent attack of rheumatism, which laid him up for a long time, causing him many sleepless nights, and leaving him unusually weak. Yet he repeatedly begged the sheik to let him depart, and supply him at least with camels to make up for the loss he had suffered from the insurrection in the town. To his great delight, two respectable Arabs offered to accompany him to Fezzán.

On the 20th of February Barth left Kúkawa, and pitched his tent on the high ground outside the city, feeling extremely happy in having at length left behind him a town of which he had become very tired.

But he was not to get off so easily; for the sheik, with whom, as with most of his kind, time was of no value, managed to hinder the traveller. At last, seeing his determination, the sheik sent five camels, which, though of inferior quality, enabled Barth to set out. But still there was delay, as the sheik earnestly desired Barth to return to the town, promising him the fulfilment of all his claims. Anxious to leave on good terms with the chief, the traveller went into the town again, but declined to stay, as his health rendered it necessary that he should at once return home. Expecting to be hindered yet a couple of months if he remained in the town, he offered to wait outside the city for a few days longer, and if the sheik should wish to see him, to come to the residence every day. To this the sheik agreed, and the two parted in the most quiet and satisfactory manner, and it appeared as if everything were arranged. Accordingly our traveller purchased two more camels, and on the 25th engaged a guide, paying him half his salary in advance.

But when all seemed ready for departure, again a message came from the sheik ordering Barth to return. He did so very reluctantly, and found that the chief was unwilling to let him depart unsatisfied. Meanwhile a large caravan had arrived from the north, bringing, among other things, money for the English mission; addressed, however, not to Dr. Barth, who had been given up as lost, but to Mr. Vogel. This made Barth's position still more unpleasant; for, instead of leaving the country honourably, he was now considered as almost disgraced by those who had sent him, the command seeming to have been taken from him and given to another and a younger man. This still further delayed his departure, and it was not until the 4th of May that Barth finally left the town and encamped outside the gate. There he waited some days for a fellow-traveller, Kolo, who was still detained in the town, and so did not take leave of the sheik until the 9th of the month.

"He received me," says Barth, "with great kindness, but was by no means backward in begging for several articles to be sent to him, especially a small cannon; which was rather out of comparison with the poor present which he had bestowed upon myself."

Just before setting out, Barth lost three camels, so that he was obliged to throw away several things, with which his people had overladen his animals.

The final start was made on the 10th of May, in a heavy thunder-storm. But nevertheless, Barth says, "I was filled with the hope that a merciful Providence would allow me to reach home in safety, in order to give a full account of my labours and discoveries."

The first night of their march was somewhat disturbed by the noise and cries of three monkeys which Barth wished to take to Europe. They so frightened the camels that they started off at a gallop, breaking several things, amongst others a strong musket. Nothing could be done but to let loose the malicious little creatures; which, instead of remaining quiet, amused themselves with loosening all the ropes with which the luggage was tied on to the backs of the animals.

At Bedwáram (where poor Macguire was probably afterwards killed) the travellers stopped for supplies of water, but had great trouble in opening the well. Then followed a tedious night march through the dreary desert of Tintumma, where Barth, lingering too long over a cup of coffee, got left behind, and would probably have had some difficulty in rejoining the caravan, had not the servants, contrary to his orders to spare the powder as much as possible, kept firing their pistols off at random. Cheered by the firing, and perhaps impressed with the awful character of the country through which they were travelling at such an hour, the slaves, forgetful of their over-fatigue, kept up an uninterrupted song, which reached the ears of Barth as he followed at some distance. When their leader did at last overtake them, the servants and slaves would fain have lagged behind, being very weary, and Barth had trouble in urging them on, to prevent them falling a sacrifice to thirst and fatigue.

At the beautiful well of Dibbela (which, however, contains abominable water), Mr. Henry Warrington, who had accompanied Vogel to Kúkawa, fell ill of dysentery—probably the result of the heat and the bad water.

After much weary travelling over sandy deserts under scorching suns, Barth at length approached Tripoli. Very pleasant were the kind messages awaiting him, and most welcome to the exhausted traveller was the sight of the wide expanse of sea, which in the bright southern sunshine spreads out with a tint of the darkest blue. He thus describes his feelings:—

"I felt so grateful to Providence for having again reached in safety the border of the Mediterranean basin, the cradle of European civilization, which from an early period had formed the object of my earnest longings and most serious course of studies, that I would fain have alighted from my horse on the sea-beach to offer up a prayer of thanksgiving to the Almighty, who, with the most conspicuous mercy, had led me through the many dangers which surrounded my path, both from fanatical men and an unhealthy climate."

Having stayed four days in Tripoli, where he was warmly welcomed by many friends, Barth embarked in a Turkish steamer returning to Malta. There he reëmbarked, and landing at Marseilles, passed through Paris, and reached London on the 6th September, where he was kindly received by Lord Palmerston and Lord Clarendon, who took the greatest interest in hearing of the remarkable success that had attended his expedition. He had been absent from Europe nearly five and a half years. The whole expedition had cost the Government a sum under £1,400.

Barth had indeed good reason to be thankful for the good fortune that had attended him. The mere fact of his having entered and left Timbuctoo alive and unharmed was in itself a remarkable proof of his zeal and perseverance.

His discoveries had been many and valuable, and afforded much new information about the past history and present condition, manners, customs, and distinctions of the various tribes of Central Africa, both Arab and Negro. But his grand discovery was that concerning the Niger—"the great highway of West Central Africa," as he aptly named it. He succeeded in exploring that part of the river left unknown by the untimely fate of Mungo Park. It is to Dr. Barth that we owe the discovery that the Benué is a tributary of the Niger, and that by it European boats can reach the regions bordering on Lake Tchad.

Not only did Barth succeed in making known a part of Africa hitherto unknown even to most Arab merchants, but he also contrived to establish friendly relations with all the most powerful chiefs along the river, up even to the mysterious city of Timbuctoo.

For Britain Dr. Barth's discoveries have a special importance; for, by showing the friendly feelings of the negro states towards England, they pointed a way to a great field for missionary enterprise, and the ending of the disgraceful traffic in slaves. It seems that the sovereigns of Central Africa, when pressed by debts which they cannot otherwise meet, or eager to obtain arms and gunpowder, endeavour to capture the black bullion of the country, which they sell to the Americans, or exchange for the instruments of war. Dr. Barth thinks that if these native princes could be got to understand that Europeans are willing to exchange the European goods for cotton, rice, and such useful products, doubtless those commodities would be more cultivated, and peace take the place of war.

CHAPTER VIII.

MR. THOMPSON ON THE NIGER.

AMONG recent African travellers Mr. Joseph Thompson takes high and honourable rank. He was second in command of the expedition which Mr. Keith Johnston led; and when that gentleman met his untimely death at the very outset of his enterprise, the journey was carried on by Mr. Thompson to a successful close. This was the beginning of young Thompson's career as an explorer, which has since gone on with increasing results and distinction. The traveller is still a young man, and, if life be spared to him, may be expected to do yet more signal work in Africa. His book, "Through Masailand," was received with marked favour by the press and the public, and at once placed the author in the foremost rank of African explorers.

The writer of these pages had the pleasure of meeting Mr. Thompson shortly after his return from one of his African journeys, and of hearing from the young traveller's own lips many interesting and curious details of life and pioneer work in Central Africa. We particularly remember Mr. Thompson's remarks as to the strange fascination which African travel exerts for all who have ever had experience of it;—how, in spite of the innumerable hardships and daily perils that must be encountered, in spite of the deadly nature of the climate and the certainty of the traveller suffering more or less from its poison, the charm of African travel still remains irresistible, luring back the explorer again and again, though he knows all the while that every new expedition probably cuts years off his life.

One of Mr. Thompson's latest journeys was along the course of the Niger to the central Soudan. As being *germane* to our subject, and an appropriate conclusion to this brief story of the Niger, we purpose giving an epitome of his experiences of a region which the labours, the heroism, and the death of many brave men have now rendered almost classic ground.

Mr. Thompson left Liverpool for the African coast in February 1885, and after touching at Madeira, Teneriffe, and Canary, landed at Bathurst on the Gambia river. Here the young traveller did not fail to visit the house which Mungo Park occupied while preparations were in train for his great journey. We may imagine what absorbing interest this spot would have for Mr. Thompson; for here were forged the beginnings of the long chain of African exploration in which Mungo Park was the first link, and Mr.

Thompson himself among the latest. Who will be the last, final link, and at what date he will fall, who may say?

From Bathurst the traveller journeyed to Sierra Leone, which he describes as the chief centre of illumination for the Dark Continent. That is to say, the people of Sierra Leone regard themselves as decidedly persons of distinction, intellectually speaking; and Mr. Thompson gives us a rapid but amusing glimpse of the Sierra Leone "nigger," promenading himself in pants of the latest Parisian mode, an astonishing expanse of snow-white linen, stove-pipe hat cocked jantily over his nose, and flourishing the trimmest of canes in his dusky hand—altogether putting on an amount of "weather-helm," as sailors say, that to the stranger is highly edifying.

Mr. Thompson's first glimpse of the Niger was the reverse of alluring. "Everything looked miserable and dreary—a steaming atmosphere, rain, thunder, lightning, and the most threatening of clouds." To right and left the eye of the traveller rested on nought but interminable expanses of mangroves, between which monotonous walls the great river stretched forward in long reaches, discoloured and gloomy in hue, and throwing out numerous arms this way and that—a depressing vista that summoned up dreary visions of fever and ague, and the innumerable physical ills that dog the footsteps of the white man in Africa.

Mr. Thompson had visited many places which disputed for the honour of being the true "white man's grave," but his first view of the Niger went far to convince him that, as the advertisements say, "none other was genuine."

At Akassa, the headquarters of the National African Company, whose servant Mr. Thompson for the time being was, the traveller's sea-journey ended. A beach strewn with the hulls of old ships and steamers, an old timber jetty, and a new iron one in course of construction, and behind these the residences of the merchants, looking pleasantly cool beneath their broad verandas, the whole framed in by the mangrove woods —such are the general features of Akassa. Mr. Thompson was hospitably welcomed and entertained by the palm-oil merchants of the depôt, the kindliness of his reception going a considerable way towards raising his spirits from the depression which his first glimpses of the Niger had induced.

We next behold the traveller fairly afloat on the great river, his means of transit being the National African Company's steam-launch *Français*. His physical feelings are not enviable; for to the intense heat of the atmosphere is added the circumstance that he sits close alongside the boilers, so that he is all the time very much like a man in a Turkish bath against his will. But the scene which feasted the traveller's eyes in a great measure compensated for the discomfort of his bodily sensations. His first unfavourable impressions of the Niger had now disappeared—no longer did he view it as the white man's sepulchre. In place of the gloomy swamps, miasma-breathing marshes, and fever-laden air which characterize the entrance of the river, his gaze now rested on magnificent virgin forests of silk-cotton and palm-oil trees. Here, the *Français* glided past little hamlets of square-shaped huts set in plantations of cocoa-nut trees; there, clearings planted with sugar-cane, beans, and yams. Naked boys sported in the warm waters in the vicinity of the villages, who shouted and laughed as the steamer drew near; women carrying water from the river swelled the hubbub, while others came flying out from the houses to watch the steamer pass. Some of the men, with an eye to business, put off in their canoes and offered fish for sale to the travellers, while others quietly watched the *Français* from the shore unmoved and unexcited; and Mr. Thompson could not help thinking of the old days of African travel, when such an invasion of the black man's territory as he was now making would have been met at the spear-point.

In these Niger hamlets all the work of the field seemed to be borne by the women, and our travellers constantly beheld groups of them preparing palm oil and engaged in other plantation work. The scenery of the river changed continually as the little launch followed its windings. Now it twisted and coiled in serpent-like folds, now it broadened into a flashing lake, girdled with yellow sand and framed in by the primeval forest. Huts dotted the banks, canoes paddled up and down the stream, a fresh breeze blew in the face of the travellers, and in this wise the *Français* pursued her voyage towards the Soudan gaily enough.

Now and then an incident of a more stirring character befell—such as the appearance of a hippopotamus. A shout from the lookout-man, a sudden snatching up of rifles, and a hurrying to get sight of the formidable river-horse! But before aim can be taken the unwieldy creature has gone down again, leaving nothing behind him but a grunt, and Master Hippo is not to be caught " this trip," as they say in Australia.

On the fourth day of the *Français'* voyage, the travellers (Mr. Thompson was accompanied by two comrades) were able to form a just estimate of the full breadth and volume of the majestic river whose course they were following. The height of the banks was now between twenty and thirty feet, the stretch of gleaming river and golden sand between being from one mile to a mile and a half in extent.

Evidences of trade now met the gaze on every hand. Every mile or two a very practical-looking factory, with unæsthetic galvanized iron roof and whitewashed walls, broke the dense greenery of the forest. Every year the stillness of the woods is being more and more disturbed by the whistle of the steamer; every year the leopard and the monkey are driven further back into their forest fastnesses. The Niger, as an exciting arena of sport and hairbreadth adventure, is yearly getting the romance knocked out of it. Reflecting upon all which, Mr. Thompson, who, we suspect, is more of a traveller and a sportsman, after all, than a trader, could not suppress a sigh. Disembarking at the residence of an "agent," he was greeted by gentlemen fashionably set forth in linen of the whitest and shiniest, and escorted into a house appointed with mahogany English furniture, while summer-houses and sunflowers were among the amenities of the surrounding gardens. Finally, a dinner of European quality, and more than European abundance, was spread for the stranger's entertainment.

This was all very pleasant and comfortable, but it was hardly this phase of life on the Niger that Mr. Thompson was desirous of studying. As soon as possible, therefore, he betook himself to the contemplation of natural man as he manifests himself on the Niger. Here again he was fated to disenchantment. The once wild and untutored black man, who had at least a sort of savage grandeur and picturesqueness, is now a "nigger" merely, passes the time of day to the stranger, and wears a lawn-tennis hat emblazoned with the self-same device with which young English tennis dandies delight to broider theirs—the ubiquitous sunflower. Indeed, this unmistakable note of an æsthetic civilization notwithstanding, the negroes of the Niger are at present poor and wretched creatures, half-starved in body and worn down by incessant civil feuds and warfare. But there are signs, Mr. Thompson tells us, that a brighter future is in store for these races, when the British Government shall have become firmly established as the protectors of the region.

And here it is fitting to note a change which took place in Mr. Thompson's opinion in regard to the effect of trade and civilization on the Niger. At first he was disposed to think that the chief result of the white man's commerce with the natives of the Niger had been to inoculate them with a love of strong drink, the disastrous effects of which were abundantly manifest on the coast settlements. But as he journeyed further up the river, he was glad to notice a vast improvement on this point. He found large stores filled with European cloth and hardware destined for the native population, while the stock of gin and other ardent liquors was by comparison very small. The African Company alone is to be thanked for this new and admirable departure, and it is doing all in its power to retrieve the evil done under the former system of trading.

After halting awhile at Lokoja, where he was joined

by Mr. W. J. Seago, a gentleman who had passed seven years on the Niger, Mr. Thompson resumed his journey. The river was now flowing through a deep valley, banked by precipitous cliffs. The scenery was in parts romantic, and the heat "simply terrific." On March 31st Egga was reached, a considerable town, and here an interpreter joined the expedition. At Shunga, where Mr. Forbes the naturalist had died a short time before, Mr. Thompson was much interested in the Yoruba men and the Nupé women traders, and especially in the enormous quantity of clothing worn by both. A Yoruba merchant's pants consume fifteen yards of cotton cloth, his coat rather more, his turban thirty yards; throw in ten yards for superfluous adornment, and you have seventy yards of cloth in all. Here, as Mr. Thompson suggests, is a magnificent field for European enterprise—where forty millions of African negroes shall require garments of this voluminous character.

Shunga was the last of the trading stations in the track of the expedition. Mr. Thompson now anticipated, being quite beyond the pale of civilization, "stirring times." He got them, but not quite of the sort he had calculated on. He and Mr. Seago were for some little time kept remarkably busy, but not by adventures with wild animals and wilder natives, but by dissension and mutiny among his own men. From threatening to murder their leaders, several of the native followers actually proceeded to the attempt, and in one instance just missed being successful. These acts of rebellion and outrage had, of course, to be met with the sternest remedies, and Mr. Thompson and Mr. Seago had literally to fight the more insubordinate of their men hand to hand. The struggle for final mastery was a desperate one, but at last victory lay with the white men; and their swarthy antagonists were taught that respect for their leaders without which such an expedition as Mr. Thompson had in hand must inevitably end in shipwreck.

The journey now led almost due north as far as Kontokora. Fresh hardships soon overtook the little party. One of Mr. Thompson's comrades, who was in front with an advance guard, broke his leg, and had to be sent back; supplies of food were difficult to be obtained through the obstinacy of native chiefs; and lastly, a terrific tornado broke over the camp. The tents were wrecked, and in the confusion and dreadful darkness which accompanied the storm the horses took fright and broke away from their fastenings. Day dawned to find the party in the most miserable case. A dozen porters and half the horse-boys had deserted; and with their numerical strength thus diminished, and after much delay in recapturing the horses, the expedition again moved forward.

A halt was made towards noon, and aid was procured at Bukani for the more exhausted of the natives.

The expedition had marched all the morning fasting, and all were at the end of their physical resources. Food was now obtained, however, and the night was passed in the midst of a second furious tornado. Next day the outlook did not brighten. The men, wearied by the march and exhausted from insufficient food, again showed signs of mutiny. They declared that unless they were provided with fish and rice they would give up the march. To procure rice and fish was a difficult and expensive matter. The Brassmen were those who were most unreasonable in their demands and most obstinate in their refusal to work. These were finally told that they might desert if they cared or dared. They did not dare, for retreat had now more risk in it than advance. Next morning the remainder of the horse-boys deserted, and Mr. Thompson and Mr. Seago had now to be their own grooms.

Every day matters looked more gloomy. Food continued to be difficult to procure, and the rebellious spirit in the camp broke out again and again. Much to the regret and chagrin of Mr. Thompson, his work at this time was little better than that of a slave-driver. But it was either this or a total abandonment of the expedition and inglorious retreat to the coast.

Amid these many and various harassments and annoyances, Mr. Thompson was nevertheless not entirely without solace. On the whole the march itself was not a difficult or toilsome one, but led by winding ways through pine forest land, thickly set with shea-butter trees. Everywhere the vegetation was of tropical wealth, and lush-green in its luxuriance; the vivid emeralds varied, however, by tints of gold and copper, like an English autumn coppice. Neither was water wanting to complete the landscape—bright streams bubbling through the forest alleys, about whose marge the palm-oil trees clustered in shady clumps. Large towns in complete ruin were here and there passed, and now and then a clearing. If the reader will turn back upon these pages, he will find Clapperton making mention of cities, with populations of tens of thousands, scattered about the same region of Northern Nupé; and Mr. Thompson, beholding these ruins, could not but reflect on their lost prosperity with sadness. For then this land was a rich and bountiful one, and the peoples of these ruined towns enjoyed life after their own rude free fashion, with feast, song, and dance. Civil war has wrought the miserable change, and the populations of these once flourishing towns are dead, or worse—sold into slavery. Everywhere Mr. Thompson saw the wreck of what had once been fertile fields. Since his journey, let it be added, Nupé has been placed under a British protectorate, and its people may now expect at least immunity from their oppressors.

As the expedition drew near Kontokora, which is

a considerable town, Mr. Thompson and Mr. Seago advanced to the front. Presently strains of wild music fell upon their ears—the music of pipes and trumpets and tom-toms. Then a company of horsemen were seen—Filianis who had ridden forth to meet the strangers. With a wild shout, the horsemen bore down upon the white men, each cavalier brandishing aloft his spear, and all gorgeously arrayed in Oriental fashion, with trappings of leather, cloth, and brass, and turbans of the most voluminous description. So warlike was the appearance of these Filiani cavalry, that Mr. Thompson at first judged their intentions to be hostile; but this was only the national manner of salute. Two venerable old men were now beheld seated beneath a tree, to whom the white men, concluding them to be persons of degree, advanced, and were received with much ceremony and many compliments. Amid a renewed uproar of shouting, and music of the pipes and tom-toms, Mr. Thompson was then conducted to Kontokora. Crowds lined the streets to witness the advent of the white men whose coming was expected, and amid a surprising show of state and pomp the strangers were escorted to the house which had been prepared for their reception, and where an abundant feast had been spread for their refreshment. This hospitable reception inspired Mr. Thompson with the hope that the worst of his difficulties were over.

A NUPÉ VILLAGE.

Page 337.

After staying two days at Kontokora, the march was resumed in a north-westerly direction, and the Niger was again struck near the Boussa Falls, the spot, our reader may remember, where Park met his death. The course of the river was followed as far as its tributary the Gulbi-n-Gindi, along which the expedition then proceeded. Here Mr. Thompson was struck down with severe sickness, which was like to end seriously, had not the course of the malady at last yielded to the treatment before reaching the most acute stage. He had hardly recovered from this illness when a desperate attempt was made on his life by one of his men, happily rendered unsuccessful by the prompt assistance of Mr. Seago. After this the mutinous spirit, which had so often broken out in the camp, died away. Awed at length by the firm, unyielding front presented by the white men, the natives "caved in," and henceforth obedience and order were maintained among Kruboys and Brassmen.

The most important town on the Gulbi-n-Gindi is Jega, a large trade centre, where converge "the main lines of commerce from the countries to the south, especially Nupé and Yoruba." At Jega, a place which was full of interest for Mr. Thompson, he could only remain one day. On the following the camp again took the road, striking westward for Sokoto. It was now towards the close of the dry season, all surrounding nature showed every sign of long drought, and the barren land and the fierce sun rendered the march difficult and painful. The land was not entirely treeless, however—fan-palms, bas-bats, and dûm-palms springing up here and there in the otherwise sterile waste. The aspect of the country was different, in many essentials, from that through which Mr. Thompson's journey had hitherto lain. No traces of civil war were anywhere manifest, no trackless forests, the home of wild beasts only, no malarious swamps and fever-haunted marshes. The earth, broken on every hand by furrow-marks, clearly showed that it was annually cultivated. Presently, too, numerous villages were met with, each containing some two or three thousand inhabitants. These hamlets were snugly enough built, the roofs of the huts being of a conical shape, the houses themselves being invariably shaded by trees.

The road now presented a busy scene of traffic and general activity. Abundant signs of commerce met the travellers; camels, donkeys, bullocks, and horses, all heavily laden, maintaining an endless stream along the highways. Filiani horsemen, looking very imposing in their picturesque and voluminous dress, ambled past, followed by numerous attendants, some on horseback, some on foot. Bringing up the rear came the ladies of the harem, veiled to the eyes from the vulgar sight—a merciful provision for the European traveller, Mr. Thompson hints, for he is thus spared

FILIANI NOBLEMAN AND ATTENDANTS.

Page 342.

the sight of some very plain faces. The people who struck Mr. Thompson as the most picturesque of any which he met in the Soudan were the Tuareg of Asben, who, clad, if such a word could be applied to them, in a very wreck of tatters and rags, contrived to fold their dirty and squalid garments around them with a wonderful picturesqueness, and to group themselves in graceful and artistic attitudes.

The religious fervour of the races among which Mr. Thompson was now sojourning was manifest on every hand. Everywhere by the roadside "praying-places" were built—little niches facing Mecca-wards—where the faithful disciples of Mohammed might at any time worship their prophet.

On May 21st the important city of Sokoto was approached. Here Mr. Thompson anticipated a ceremonious reception; to be worthy of which he and Mr. Seago arrayed themselves in their most gorgeous attire. The leader of the expedition made himself gorgeous in a parti-coloured singlet of silk and wool, white ducks, canvas gaiters, and puggaree-enveloped helmet; while Mr. Seago was got up in pyjamas, white jacket, helmet and gaiters. What was the particular significance of the gaiters—an uncomfortable article in a warm climate—Mr. Thompson does not tell us, but they were probably donned with an eye to some possible effect on the native mind.

At first the reception of the travellers at Sokoto

was the reverse of what had been looked for; but this, they presently heard, was due to the circumstance that their guide had been procured from an enemy of the governor. Before long, Mr. Thompson and his companions were provided with an abundance of food, both cooked and uncooked, by the leading men of the city.

On the day following his arrival at Sokoto, and while messengers were on their way to the sultan, Mr. Thompson employed the time in taking photographs. He was thus drawn into an adventure, disagreeable in its details, and coming very near to being disastrous in its consequences. The traveller set up his camera in the market-place, then in the full tide of trade, with an uproar filling the air from some tens of thousands of bargaining and disputing traders. None of these people had ever seen a white man before, and when one came armed with so curious a looking instrument as a photographic camera, it is little to be wondered at that the crowd took fright at the phenomenon. The throng pressed closer and closer about Mr. Thompson; cries arose which presently swelled into a deafening shout, every moment growing angrier and more excited. The camera very nearly came to grief. The incensed and agitated mob pressed on; the market stalls were knocked over, and their contents scattered on the ground. Sheep, goats, cattle, and camels, got loose, and rushing about among the crowd, made confusion thrice confounded; and in

VIEW IN SOKOTO.   Page 366.

the midst of this extraordinary scene of panic and uproar the white men, for a little, fared very badly. At last they succeeded in pushing their way through the throng and getting free of the market-place. The people had got it into their heads that the photographic apparatus was an instrument of witchcraft, and that Mr. Thompson's intention was to exercise its powers upon them.

On the following day the travellers presented themselves before the sultan Umuru Serki-n-Musulmia. Passing through a court and passage, they were escorted to a massively-built, flat-roofed edifice, in front of which stood an elevated throne of mud. Here sat, cross-legged and robed in a mantle broidered with gold thread, the sultan himself. Nothing of his face was visible except a pair of flashing eyes; and so motionless did Umuru sit that he looked most like a figure of a Buddhist god.

Elaborate salutations having passed between the sultan and the white men, followed by a series of endless interrogations on Umuru's part, they at last came to business, and Mr. Thompson detailed the object of his mission. First he thanked the sultan for the friendly spirit he had always displayed towards English traders on the river, and begged to present a small token of their appreciation of the monarch's kindness. The Englishmen were desirous of entering into a treaty with Umuru, whereby the relations between the two might be placed upon a proper footing and strengthened by every means possible. In this way great commercial and other advantages would accrue, not only to the English traders, but in an equal degree to the sultan.

To all Mr. Thompson's arguments Umuru listened with close attention and marked signs of approval; greatly, of course, to the satisfaction of the former. At the conclusion of the white man's speech the sultan expressed himself delighted at the idea of being brought into closer communication with England and Englishmen; and at this point Mr. Thompson deemed it politic to clinch matters by displaying the presents he had brought for the negro monarch's acceptance. These were accordingly brought on the evening of the same day, and proved to be of the most varied and gorgeous description. At first Umuru affected to contemplate the white men's gift with a dignified calm; but this presently broke down utterly as the magnificence of the present—costly beyond his utmost expectation—became fully realized. Beautiful fabrics in satin, silk, and velvet, gorgeous embroideries, rugs, silver-mounted fire-arms, silver cups, etc., and all of the finest workmanship, were displayed before his delighted eyes; and lastly, a wonderful silk umbrella, of the largest dimensions and deeply fringed with gold cord, took complete possession of the royal heart, and Umuru gave vent to the liveliest expressions of his surprise and pleasure.

On the following day Mr. Thompson presented the treaty with which he was charged to the sultan, for his consideration and approval. This document showed forth how "concessions and grants must be made on the one hand, if wealth and increased influence and power were to be secured on the other." Umuru considered all the proposals contained in the treaty with more than readiness, and finally signed the document with alacrity. Mr. Thompson's enterprise was thus brought to a successful termination with a greater degree of ease and expedition than he had ever allowed himself to hope. Handsome presents were made to the chief men belonging to the sultan's court, and Mr. Thompson left Sokoto for Gandu to negotiate a second treaty there.

While sojourning in the Central Soudan, Mr. Thompson found leisure in the midst of his commercial negotiations to note the many novel and curious sights that hourly presented themselves before him. All these were of an exceedingly interesting character; the "negro empires of the Soudan being so unique and remarkable in their various characteristics that one is kept in a continual state of surprise, not less by what is indigenous than by what is foreign and imported from North Africa."

Mr. Thompson was, as has been indicated, the agent of the African Company during the expedition which we have just sketched. It will therefore be *germane* to our subject if we give here a brief summary of the work and aims of the African Company, or, as it is now called, the "National African Company."

In 1829 the course of the Lower Niger had been followed into the Gulf of Guinea, and in that year it seemed as if a new history awaited the Central Soudan, which had up to this date been barred to European mercantile enterprise. But for thirty years all attempts to establish commercial relations with this region proved fruitless. Life and money were freely spent in the enterprise, in every case with disastrous results. Then the British Government withdrew all official help in the matter, and the adventure fell into private hands. One firm after another planted trading depôts along the Niger, and the pioneer work was carried on by various leaders, notable among whom was Mr. James Croft, once known as the "Father of the Niger." Nevertheless security of life and property was not as yet assured, and it was felt by all interested in the enterprise that some kind of political organization was needed to secure this.

In the days antecedent to the establishment of the private trading stations above referred to, all the region of Central Africa with which we are dealing was the arena of continual inter-tribal warfare and slave raids; and when to this is added the circumstance that the various British firms were brought into frequent rivalry, and that there was the want of anything like unity of action among the white traders, it can easily be understood how progress was slow and unsatisfactory. But in 1879 all the British interests on the Niger joined their forces, and the "United African Company" was the result. One leading feature in the plan of action of the new company was the endeavour to unite the numerous heterogeneous tribes into one compact whole. It was resolved at the same time that the company should interfere as little as possible with the merely internal affairs of each separate tribe. The company proved successful both in a political and in a financial view. Its objects were political and commercial development, the former as a means to the latter; the endeavour to effect this development by the agency of a single company, so as to avoid intrigue and rivalry; and to bring the empires of Gandu and Sokoto into immediate relations with the company, and thus in time include the territories of the Tchad basin within the company's operations.

In 1882 the British Government granted the company a royal charter, and its name now became the "National African Company." The enterprise received a marked stimulus from the grant of the charter—new steamers and launches were built, new depôts established, while small stations became large and important ones. Thus the company prospered, until two French houses took up the ground, and entered into rivalry with it. Had their opponents confined themselves to purely commercial work, the African Company could have had no reason for complaint. But this the French houses did not do. They used every endeavour to secure political influence over the native princes; and a scheme was set on foot, under the auspices of M. Gambetta, for welding Tunis, Algeria, Senegal, the Central Soudan, and the Lower Niger into a Franco-African empire. The idea was a sufficiently comprehensive one, and whatever its practical results might have been, it would have effected this at least—namely, the death-blow of the National African Company. The French operations on the Niger continued to develop, and had now to be met by greatly increased activity, and a large outlay of money on the part of the company. It was clear that the two rival parties could not exist side by side, and the African Company was resolved that it should not be the one to go to the wall. This region was indebted in every way to British enterprise and British money, and no one can wonder at the position which the company took up in the circumstances. The struggle was a sharp one, but in the end the older company was left master of the situation. One of the two French houses disappeared from the scene, while the other became absorbed in the English company. But now a new danger arose for the African Company. Germany conceived the idea of colonization, for the first time in her history. At this time there existed in Germany a feeling strongly antagonistic to England, and it was probably altogether congenial to the nation that it should endeavour to press forward colonizing operations in Africa. Into the fresh struggle which thus arose the African Company threw itself with great vigour, despatching Mr. Thompson as its envoy to the Niger, as has been described in these pages. Mr. Thompson was successful in concluding treaties with no less than two hundred and thirty-five native chiefs, as well as with the Mohammedan empires of Gandu and Sokoto.

The National African Company has been able to maintain, with little or no loss of life by violence and small loss of property, from fifty to one hundred establishments, scattered among dense populations which now engage in amicable barter with the company, where they would have once thought nothing of resorting to force. This is in itself a very notable achievement. Out of very rude and barbarous material the company has formed a fairly peaceful and orderly state; and this not by force of arms, but by the legitimate arts of commerce. That it has gained the confidence of the native races is sufficiently indicated by the fact that they have continually referred their inter-tribal disputes to the judication of the company, and that the native princes have been found ready to surrender their sovereign powers to the company. A large majority of the chiefs have now, through their relations with the company, the ambition of honestly earning their own livelihood, instead of engaging, as formerly, in unrestricted plunder, war, and slave-raids. Thus has commercial enterprise been used as a distinctly civilizing agent among the peoples of the Niger.

Here our "Story of the Niger" ends. We have traced for you, kind reader, the history of the great river from the days before Park down to the present moment: we followed that great pioneer of travel in Central Africa through the various stages of his memorable journey; and we have accompanied Clapperton and the Landers on their adventurous and notable expeditions; we have noted what valuable additions to our knowledge of the mighty river Barth's explorations yielded; we have gone with Captain Gallieni in his spirited mission; and with Mr. Joseph Thompson's interesting and successful journey the record in the meantime closes. Other travellers will doubtless follow Mr. Thompson, and in a few years' time a new Story of the Niger may have to be told. But it must necessarily be a story of a different kind from that which has been given in these pages—that is, it must become less and less a story of adventure and peril, and toil and death, and more and more a record of commercial enterprise and the spread of civilization. Every year the Niger is becoming less and less the great river of mystery and darkness which it was to the early explorers. The days of Park and Clapperton and the Landers can never return, as far as the Niger is concerned. This is a loss to the adventurer and the sportsman—to all those who in past times have regarded the Niger as a happy hunting-ground and a prolific birthplace of surprising adventures—but to the world at large, let us hope, a gain. We close with the earnest hope that the ascendency and authority, the power and the prestige, which England has secured on the Niger, may be exercised to all wise and just issues; that our commercial dealings with these poor, semi-barbarous peoples of Western and Central Africa, while stimulating and extending British industry and merchant enterprise, may be marked by no policy, by no single act, that shall leave a stain upon our name and honour.

THE END.

Boy's Library of Travel and Adventure.

The Three Trappers. A Book for Boys. By ACHILLES DAUNT, Author of "In the Land of the Moose, the Bear, and the Beaver." With 11 Engravings. Post 8vo, cloth extra. Price 3s. 6d.

A Canadian story, for young readers, beautifully illustrated, combining useful information in natural history and geography, with interesting incidents and adventures.

Wrecked on a Reef; or, Twenty Months in the Auckland Isles. A True Story of Shipwreck, Adventure, and Suffering. With 40 Illustrations. Post 8vo, cloth extra. Price 3s. 6d.

A true story of five men who were wrecked among the Auckland Isles, and escaped at last in a boat of their own building.

Egypt Past and Present. Described and Illustrated. With a Narrative of its Occupation by the British, and of Recent Events in the Soudan. By W. H. DAVENPORT ADAMS. With 100 Illustrations and Portrait of General Gordon. Post 8vo, cloth extra. Price 3s. 6d.

In this volume are brought together the principal facts in connection with the history and monuments of Egypt. The illustrations are from authentic sources.

Ralph's Year in Russia. A Story of Travel and Adventure in Eastern Europe. A Book for Boys. By ROBERT RICHARDSON, Author of "Almost a Hero," etc. With Eight Engravings. Post 8vo, cloth extra. Price 3s.

The story of an English family required for a time to reside in Russia. It introduces numerous and varied incidents of travel and adventure in that country, and describes the various customs and mode of life of the people.

Robinson Crusoe. The Life and Strange Adventures of Robinson Crusoe, of York, Mariner. Written by Himself. *Carefully Reprinted from the Original Edition.* With Memoir of De Foe, a Memoir of Alexander Selkirk, and other interesting additions. Illustrated with upwards of Seventy Engravings by KEELEY HALSWELLE. Crown 8vo, cloth extra. Price 3s.

An Edition that every boy would be pleased to include in his library. It is handsomely bound, and the numerous illustrations assist greatly in the realization of this famous story.

The Swiss Family Robinson; or, Adventures of a Shipwrecked Family on a Desolate Island. *A New and Unabridged Translation.* With upwards of 300 Engravings. Crown 8vo, cloth extra. Price 3s.

A book similar in character to the famous "Robinson Crusoe," and consequently fascinating to young readers. There is a vast amount of instructive information on natural history, etc., interwoven with the story.

Gulliver's Travels into Several Remote Regions of the World. With Introduction and Explanatory Notes by the late ROBERT MACKENZIE, Author of "The 19th Century," "America," etc. With 20 Illustrations. Post 8vo, cloth extra. Price 3s.

"A very handsome edition, under the editorship of Mr. Robert Mackenzie, who has supplied for it a well-written introduction and explanatory notes.... We have also here the curious original maps and a number of modern illustrations of much merit. Altogether this is a most attractive re-appearance of a famous book."—GLASGOW HERALD.

T. NELSON AND SONS, LONDON, EDINBURGH, AND NEW YORK.

Guide Books for Tourists.

Rambles in Rome. An Archæological and Historical Guide to the Museums, Galleries, Villas, Churches, and Antiquities of Rome and the Campagna. By S. RUSSELL FORBES, Archæological and Historical Lecturer on Roman Antiquities. Fifth Edition. Revised and enlarged; embracing all the recent excavations and discoveries. With Maps, Plans, and numerous Illustrations. Post 8vo, cloth extra. Price 3s. 6d.

"*You will find in this book a high class companion and guide.*"—C. H. SPURGEON.

Rambles in Naples. An Archæological and Historical Guide to the Museums, Galleries, Villas, Churches, and Antiquities of Naples and its Environs. By S. RUSSELL FORBES, Archæological and Historical Lecturer on Roman Antiquities; Author of "Rambles in Rome," etc. Third Edition. With Maps, Plans, and Illustrations. Post 8vo, cloth. 2s. 6d.

The Tourist's Handbook to Switzerland. With Practical Information as to Routes, Excursions, Railway and Diligence Fares, etc. By ROBERT ALLBUT, Member of the Italian Alpine Club. With 24 Maps, 6 Plans, and 25 Illustrations. Post 8vo, cloth. Price 3s. 6d.

"*As Mr. Allbut is an experienced tourist conductor, he is able to give many hints that will prove useful to the inexperienced.... On the whole this new guide may be accepted as trustworthy.*"—THE TIMES.

The Isle of Wight. Its History, Topography, and Antiquities. By W. H. DAVENPORT ADAMS. New and Revised Edition, with 16 Pages of Sectional Maps and Plans, and a Large Map of the Island printed in Colours, all from the Maps of the Ordnance Survey. 323 pages, post 8vo, cloth. Price 3s.

A Guide which exactly meets the wants of Tourists.

Books of Travel.

On the Nile. The Story of a Family Trip to the Land of Egypt. By SARA K. HUNT. With 16 Engravings. Post 8vo, cloth. Price 3s.

The scenes and customs of the country are described in a simple, interesting, and attractive manner.

Recent Expeditions to Eastern Polar Seas. With Twelve Engravings and Two Charts. Post 8vo. 1s. 6d.

CONTENTS:—*Voyage of the "Hansa," "Germania," and the "Tegethoff."*

Records of adventure and endurance in connection with research in the Polar Regions possess a never-ending charm. The narratives contained in this volume will be found as full of interest and as exciting as any of those which have preceded them.

Adventurous Boat Voyages. By ROBERT RICHARDSON, Author of "Ralph's Year in Russia," "Almost a Hero," etc. With 15 Illustrations. Post 8vo, cloth. 3s.

An interesting book, with accounts of daring and remarkable voyages in open boats, by Lieutenant Bligh, Captain Ross, Dr. Kane, Macgregor, Stanley, etc.

Rambles Through Bible Lands. By the Rev. RICHARD NEWTON, D.D. With 60 Engravings, Post 8vo, cloth extra. Price 3s.

A narrative of travels in the Holy Land, Egypt, etc. It is written in a style that will make it attractive to the young, and at the same time interesting and profitable to those of mature years.

"*A book of books for the family library.*"—SWORD AND TROWEL.

T. NELSON AND SONS, LONDON, EDINBURGH, AND NEW YORK.

Boy's Library of Travel and Adventure.

Beyond the Himalayas. A Book for Boys. By JOHN GEDDIE, F.R.G.S., Author of "The Lake Regions of Central Africa," etc. With Nine Engravings. Post 8vo, cloth extra. Price 3s. 6d.

A story of travel and adventure in the Wilds of Thibet. The book is really instructive, while it is certainly entertaining. There is scarcely one of its twenty chapters which does not contain the record of some startling adventure. The full-page woodcuts enhance the attraction of the volume for young readers.

The Castaways. A Story of Adventure in the Wilds of Borneo. By Captain MAYNE REID. Post 8vo, cloth extra. Price 3s. 6d.

Adventures of a shipwrecked party, including the captain's two children; encounters with crocodiles, gorillas, etc.

Frank Redcliffe. A Story of Travel and Adventure in the Forests of Venezuela. A Book for Boys. By ACHILLES DAUNT, Author of "The Three Trappers," etc. With numerous Illustrations. Post 8vo, cloth extra. 3s. 6d.

A tale for boys, of romantic adventure in the wild districts traversed by the Orinoco. With beautiful engravings.

In the Land of the Moose, the Bear, and the Beaver. Adventures in the Forests of the Athabasca. By ACHILLES DAUNT, Author of "The Three Trappers." With Illustrations. Post 8vo, cloth extra. Price 3s. 6d.

The adventures of three hunters, one an old trapper, the others Canadian youths, among the wilds of North-western Canada. The book gives an interesting description of scenery and natural history, in a narrative form, at once attractive and useful for young readers.

In the Bush and on the Trail. Adventures in the Forests of North America. A Book for Boys. By M. BENEDICT REVOIL. With 70 Illustrations. Post 8vo, cloth extra. Price 3s. 6d.

A very interesting translation from the work of a French traveller. Much valuable information given regarding natural history and scenery in an attractive form, along with beautiful engravings.

The Lake Regions of Central Africa. A Record of Modern Discovery. By JOHN GEDDIE, F.R.G.S. With 32 Illustrations. Post 8vo, cloth extra. 3s. 6d.

CONTENTS.—*Introductory and Historical—The Nile—The White Nile and the Albert Nyanza—The Ultimate Nile Sources—The Congo—Tanganyika—The Lualaba Lakes—Cataracts—The Zambesi from Lake Dilolo to Lake Ngami—The Victoria Falls and the Lower Zambesi —The Shiré and Lake Nyassa.*

Lost in the Backwoods. A Tale of the Canadian Forest. By Mrs. TRAILL, Author of "In the Forest," etc. With 32 Engravings. Post 8vo, cloth extra. 3s. 6d.

This story was many years since published under the title of "The Canadian Crusoes." It abounds with incidents of romantic adventure, and with attractive and interesting descriptions. In its new form it is sure to become a favourite with the young people of the present day.

The Meadows Family; or, Fireside Stories of Adventure and Enterprise. By M. A. PAULL, Author of "Tim's Troubles," etc. With Illustrations. Post 8vo, cloth extra, gold and colours. Price 3s. 6d.

A book of fascinating descriptions and incidents, taken from authentic records of travel and adventure in wild, picturesque regions.

T. NELSON AND SONS, LONDON, EDINBURGH, AND NEW YORK.

Pictures of Travel in Many Lands.

The Amazon and its Wonders. With Illustrations of Animal Life in the Amazonian Forest. 28 Engravings. Post 8vo, cloth extra. Price 2s.

A history of this great river and the regions through which it flows, from the earliest historical notices in the year 1500 to the accounts of recent explorers.

California and its Wonders. By the Rev. JOHN TODD, D.D. New Edition, carefully Revised and brought down to the present time. 17 Engravings. Post 8vo, cloth extra. Price 2s.

Full of interesting and instructive matter. The engravings well depict the natural wonders described in the text.

The Euphrates and the Tigris. A Narrative of Discovery and Adventure. With a Description of the Ruins of Babylon and Nineveh. 18 Engravings. Post 8vo, cloth extra. Price 2s.

A narrative of modern discoveries in the lands of Babylon and Nineveh; the excavations by Layard, the inscriptions deciphered by Smith, etc., etc.

Famous Caverns and Grottoes. Described and Illustrated. By W. H. DAVENPORT ADAMS. With 38 Illustrations. Post 8vo, cloth extra. Price 2s.

An interesting volume, beautifully illustrated, describing the most remarkable caverns and grottoes of our globe under five classes:—those of volcanic origin, those excavated by water, stalactite caves, ice caves, and caves full of fossil remains.

Famous Caves and Catacombs. Described and Illustrated. By W. H. DAVENPORT ADAMS. With 40 Illustrations. Post 8vo, cloth extra. Price 2s.

A beautiful volume, containing a mass of information and description regarding the ancient cave-temples of Egypt and Hindostan, the grottoes and caverns of Greece and Italy, and the catacombs of Rome and Paris. With many illustrations from drawings or photographs.

The French in Indo-China. With 33 Engravings. Post 8vo, cloth extra. Price 2s.

A narrative of Garnier's explorations and adventures in Cochin-China, Cambodia, Laos, and Siam, with a history of the origin of the French colony in Cochin-China, and an account of the events which resulted in the recent difficulties between China and France.

Gibraltar and its Sieges. With a Description of its Natural Features. 18 Engravings. Post 8vo, cloth extra. Price 2s.

A new account of the great Rock-Fortress, carefully prepared and illustrated. The celebrated work by Colonel Drinkwater, on the siege in 1782, is largely made use of, and several of his plates are given in facsimile on a reduced scale.

In the Forest; or, Pictures of Life and Scenery in the Wilds of Canada. By Mrs. TRAILL, Author of "Lost in the Backwoods," etc. With numerous Illustrations. Post 8vo, cloth extra. 2s.

Contains much pleasant information, and many interesting anecdotes regarding the plants and animals of Canada, and some lively details of Indian life.

Round the World. A Story of Travel compiled from the Narrative of Ida Pfeiffer. By D. MURRAY SMITH. 36 Engravings. Post 8vo, cloth extra. Price 2s.

Madame Pfeiffer's great powers of observation enabled her well to describe all that was striking and pleasing connected with the people and countries through which she passed.

Madame Ida Pfeiffer. The Story of Ida Pfeiffer, and Her Travels in Many Lands. 25 Engravings. Post 8vo, cloth extra. Price 2s.

A new biography of this remarkable lady, the boldest of female travellers, who, with daring such as no woman had ever shown before, ventured alone into savage lands, studying the manners and customs of their inhabitants.

T. NELSON AND SONS, LONDON, EDINBURGH, AND NEW YORK.

Travel and Adventure.

Jack Hooper. His Adventures at Sea and in South Africa. By VERNEY LOVETT CAMERON, C.B., D.C.L., Commander Royal Navy; Author of "Across Africa," "Our Future Highway," etc. With 23 Full-page Illustrations. Crown 8vo, cloth extra, gilt edges. 5s.

"Our author has the immense advantage over many writers of boys' stories that he describes what he has seen, and does not merely draw on his imagination and on books."—SCOTSMAN.

With Pack and Rifle in the Far South-West. Adventures in New Mexico, Arizona, and Central America. By ACHILLES DAUNT, Author of "Frank Redcliffe," "In the Land of the Moose, the Bear, and the Beaver," "The Three Trappers," etc. With 30 Illustrations. Crown 8vo, cloth extra, gilt edges. 5s.

A delightful book of travel and adventure, with much valuable information as to the geography and natural history of the wild American "Far West."

The Eastern Archipelago. By the Author of "The Arctic World," "Recent Polar Voyages," etc. With 60 Engravings and a Map. Crown 8vo, cloth extra, gilt edges. Price 5s.

A description of the scenery, animal and vegetable life, people, and physical wonders of the islands in the Eastern Seas.

Early English Voyagers; or, The Adventures and Discoveries of Drake, Cavendish, and Dampier. Numerous Illustrations. Crown 8vo, cloth extra, gilt edges. 5s.

The title of this work describes the contents. It is a handsome volume, which will be a valuable gift for young persons generally, and boys in particular. There are included many interesting illustrations and portraits of the three great voyagers.

Our Sea Coast Heroes; or, Tales of Wreck and of Rescue by the Lifeboat and Rocket. By ACHILLES DAUNT, Author of "Frank Redcliffe," "With Pack and Rifle in the Far South-West," etc. With numerous Illustrations. Post 8vo, cloth extra. 2s. 6d.

The Forest, the Jungle, and the Prairie; or, Tales of Adventure and Enterprise in Pursuit of Wild Animals. With numerous Engravings. Post 8vo, cloth extra. Price 2s. 6d.

A party of weather-bound schoolboys are here supposed to relate in turn the stories that form the book. They are full of romantic adventure and deeds of daring; but at the same time they are true, and cannot be read without imparting valuable information on natural history.

Scenes with the Hunter and the Trapper in Many Lands. Stories of Adventures with Wild Animals. With Engravings. Post 8vo, cloth extra. Price 2s. 6d.

A party of school-boys spend some of their half-holidays in relating to one another stories of adventure in search of wild animals. These stories, though often full of romantic and stirring incidents, are all true. They cannot fail to be attractive to young readers.

The Swiss Family Robinson; or, Adventures of a Father and his Four Sons on a Desolate Island. Illustrated. Post 8vo, cloth extra. Price 2s. 6d.

A cheap edition of this well-known work. As the title suggests, its character is somewhat similar to that of the famous "Robinson Crusoe." It combines, in a high degree, the two desirable qualities in a book,—instruction and amusement.

Sandford and Merton. A Book for the Young. By THOMAS DAY. Illustrated. Post 8vo, cloth extra. Price 2s. 6d.

T. NELSON AND SONS, LONDON, EDINBURGH, AND NEW YORK.

R. M. Ballantyne's Books for Boys.

The Coral Island. A Tale of the Pacific. With Illustrations. Post 8vo, cloth extra. Price 3s. 6d.

The Young Fur-Traders; or, Snowflakes and Sunbeams from the Far North. With Illustrations. Post 8vo, cloth extra. Price 3s. 6d.

The World of Ice. Adventures in the Polar Regions. With Illustrations. Post 8vo, cloth extra. Price 3s. 6d.

The Gorilla Hunters. A Tale of the Wilds of Africa. With Illustrations. Post 8vo, cloth extra. Price 3s. 6d.

Martin Rattler. A Boy's Adventures in the Forests of Brazil. With Illustrations. Post 8vo, cloth extra. Price 3s. 6d.

Ungava. A Tale of Esquimau Land. With Illustrations. Post 8vo, cloth extra. Price 3s. 6d.

The Dog Crusoe and his Master. A Story of Adventure on the Western Prairies. With Illustrations. Post 8vo, cloth extra. Price 3s. 6d.

These seven lively and interesting narratives by R. M. Ballantyne form a complete repertory of good reading for young people. They give a vivid and picturesque description of various climes, and depict strange adventures in many lands.

Hudson Bay; or, Everyday Life in the Wilds of North America, during a Six Years' Residence in the Territories of the Hon. Hudson Bay Company. By R. M. BALLANTYNE. With 29 Illustrations drawn by BAYARD and other Artists, from Sketches by the Author. Post 8vo, cloth extra. Price 3s. 6d.

In this volume much useful information is communicated, in the most fascinating narrative style, about everyday life in the wilds of North America.

W. H. G. Kingston's Books for Boys.

Afar in the Forest. With 41 Full-page Engravings. Post 8vo, cloth extra. Price 3s. 6d.

A tale of settler life in North America, full of stirring adventure.

In New Granada; or, Heroes and Patriots. With 36 Full-page Engravings. Post 8vo, cloth extra. Price 3s. 6d.

A narrative of some of the episodes of the desperate struggle of which the present Republic of New Granada was the scene, before its people were able to establish their independence of Spain. Descriptions of the scenery, products, and social customs of the country are intermixed with the story.

In the Rocky Mountains. A Tale of Adventure. With 41 Engravings. Post 8vo, cloth extra. Price 3s. 6d.

A narrative of adventure in the Far West. Especially adapted to the taste and delectation of youth, with numerous incidents of travel and amusing stories, told in a fresh and invigorating style.

Kingston's Western World. Picturesque Sketches of Nature and Natural History in Northern and Central America. With 86 Engravings. By W. H. G. Kingston. Crown 8vo, cloth extra. Price 4s.

W. H. G. Kingston's Books for Boys.

In the Eastern Seas; or, The Regions of the Bird of Paradise. A Tale for Boys. With 111 Illustrations. Crown 8vo, gilt edges. Price 6s.

A tale of voyage and adventure among the islands of the Malay Archipelago, with descriptions of scenery and objects of natural history.

In the Wilds of Africa. With upwards of 70 Illustrations. Crown 8vo, gilt edges. Price 6s.

An interesting account of adventures by a shipwrecked party who are landed on the west coast of Africa, and make their way to the south through many dangers.

On the Banks of the Amazon; or, A Boy's Journal of his Adventures in the Tropical Wilds of South America. Profusely Illustrated. Crown 8vo, gilt edges. Price 6s.

In the course of the narrative some of the numberless animals, as well as a few of the most interesting of the vegetable productions, of the Amazonian Valley are described.

Saved from the Sea; or, The Loss of the *Viper*, and the Adventures of her Crew in the Great Sahara. With 30 Full-page Engravings. Crown 8vo, gilt edges. Price 5s.

A young sailor's account of his own adventures, along with three shipwrecked comrades.

The South Sea Whaler. A Story of the Loss of the *Champion*, and the Adventures of her Crew. With upwards of 30 Engravings. Crown 8vo, gilt edges. Price 5s.

A tale of mutiny and shipwreck in the South Seas, the captain having his son and daughter on board with him.

In the Wilds of Florida. With 37 Engravings. Crown 8vo, gilt edges. Price 5s.

A tale of warfare and hunting

Twice Lost. With Thirty-six Engravings. Crown 8vo, gilt edges. Price 5s.

A young sailor's story of shipwreck, and perilous adventures in the wilds of Australia.

A Voyage Round the World. A Tale for Boys. With 42 Engravings. Crown 8vo, gilt edges. Price 5s.

A young sailor's account of his own adventures by sea and land, the scenes being laid chiefly in South America, the South Sea Islands, and Japan.

Old Jack. A Sea Tale. With 66 Engravings. Crown 8vo, gilt edges. Price 5s.

An old sailor's account of his own adventures, during times of peace and of war, in many parts of the world.

The Wanderers; or Adventures in the Wilds of Trinidad and up the Orinoco. With 30 Full-page Engravings. Crown 8vo, gilt edges. Price 5s.

A Pennsylvanian merchant sets out with his family to South America, and meets with many adventures by sea and land, which are related by his son.

The Young Llanero. A Story of War and Wild Life in Venezuela. With 44 Engravings. Crown 8vo, gilt edges. Price 5s.

A thrilling and fascinating narrative of adventures in South America.

The Young Rajah. A Story of Indian Life and Adventure. With upwards of 40 Full-page Engravings. Crown 8vo, gilt edges. 5s.

A story of the Indian Mutiny; the hero a young Indian prince, who had received an English education and become a Christian.

My First Voyage to Southern Seas. With 52 Engravings. Crown 8vo, gilt edges. Price 5s.

A young sailor's story, describing Cape Colony, Ceylon, Aden, etc.

T. NELSON AND SONS, LONDON, EDINBURGH, AND NEW YORK.

Works on Nature and Natural History.

Chips from the Earth's Crust; or, Short Studies in Natural Science. By JOHN GIBSON, Natural History Department, Edinburgh Museum of Science and Art; Author of "Science Gleanings in Many Fields," etc. With 29 Illustrations. Post 8vo, cloth extra. Price 2s. 6d.

"A popular account of the Earth's surface and formation, such as may interest and instruct boys of an inquiring habit of mind. It comprises chapters on earthquakes, meteors, tornadoes, and other phenomena."—SATURDAY REVIEW.

Science Gleanings in Many Fields. By JOHN GIBSON, Natural History Department, Edinburgh Museum of Science and Art. With 18 Illustrations. Post 8vo, cloth extra. Price 2s. 6d.

The reader will find "Science Gleanings" rich in information regarding such interesting topics as animal intelligence, animal mimicry, the weapons of animals, their partnerships, and their migrations. Much information is also given regarding food fishes and about animals with which, whether as friends or foes, man has more especially to do. Glimpses of the past life of the globe are obtained in the essays on the mammoth, the great auk, and other extinct animals.

Monsters of the Sea, Legendary and Authentic. By JOHN GIBSON, Natural History Department, Edinburgh Museum of Science and Art, Author of "Science Gleanings in Many Fields," etc. With 16 Illustrations. Foolscap 8vo, cloth extra. Price 1s. 6d.

"An instructive as well as interesting little book, giving an account, not only of genuine sea monsters and the huge snakes of Brazilian rivers, but also of real or fabled appearances of the great sea-serpent that has yet to be caught."—SCOTSMAN.

In the Polar Regions; or, Nature and Natural History in the Frozen Zones. With Anecdotes and Stories of Adventure and Travel. 46 Illustrations. Post 8vo, cloth extra. Price 2s. 6d.

In the Tropical Regions; or, Nature and Natural History in the Torrid Zone. With Anecdotes and Stories of Adventure and Travel. 78 Illustrations. Post 8vo, cloth extra. 2s. 6d.

In the Temperate Regions; or, Nature and Natural History in the Temperate Zones. With Anecdotes and Stories of Adventure and Travel. 72 Illustrations. Post 8vo, cloth extra. 2s. 6d.

"In the Polar," "In the Tropical," and "In the Temperate Regions," are three companion volumes, though each is complete in itself. The full title suggests the character of the books. They are replete with information on the animal and vegetable life of the countries described, and abound in illustrations in elucidation of the text. Good books either for school or home libraries.

Gaussen's World's Birthday. Illustrated. Foolscap 8vo. 2s. 6d.

Lectures delivered to an audience of young people, in Geneva, on the first chapter of Genesis. The discoveries of astronomical and geological science are simply explained, and harmonized with the statements of Scripture.

Nature's Wonders; or, How God's Works Praise Him. By the Rev. RICHARD NEWTON, D.D. With 53 Engravings. Post 8vo. 2s. 6d.

Addresses to young persons, on various subjects of science and natural history, to show "how God's works praise him." With illustrative anecdotes and engravings.

Works on Nature and Natural History.

The Homes of the Birds. By M. K. M., Author of "The Birds We See," etc. With 65 Illustrations by GIACOMELLI. Post 8vo, cloth extra. Price 2s.
A charming book of natural history, written in a very attractive style, and illustrated by beautiful engravings.

Jenny and the Insects; or, Little Toilers and their Industries. With 26 Illustrations by GIACOMELLI. Post 8vo, cloth extra. Price 2s.
The insects are represented as telling their several histories. Any child, after reading this book, will hardly be able to pass even a spider without being reminded that the smallest insects have each and all their allotted tasks to perform.

Things in the Forest. By MARY and ELIZABETH KIRBY. With Coloured Frontispiece and Fifty Illustrations. Royal 18mo. 1s. 6d.
A book about birds; well calculated to encourage a taste for the study of the natural history of the feathered tribes.

Sea-Birds and the Lessons of their Lives. By Mrs. SURR, Author of "Good out of Evil." With 24 Illustrations by GIACOMELLI and other Artists. Post 8vo. Price 1s.
Very pleasantly does the author describe the birds and their habits, and gossip about them for the entertainment and instruction of the young.

Nature's Wonders. Pictures of Remarkable Scenes in Foreign Lands. With Coloured Frontispiece and numerous Engravings. Royal 18mo. Price 1s.
An admirable book for the school library or a school reward. The information given is full of interest, and of just the kind to make an intelligent lad anxious to pursue the study further.

What Shall We Talk About? A Book for the Young. With 34 Illustrations. Post 8vo, cloth extra. Price 2s. 6d.

Scenes of Wonder in Many Lands. Being Descriptions of Rapids, Cascades, Waterfalls, etc. With Coloured Frontispiece and numerous Engravings. Royal 18mo. Price 1s.
The natural wonders here described possess imposing or striking features, which cannot fail to make them of interest to the young reader, and to foster in him a love of reading of a kind that will add to his store of knowledge.

Wonders of Creation.—VOLCANOES AND THEIR PHENOMENA. With Coloured Frontispiece and numerous Engravings. Royal 18mo. Price 1s.
The descriptions of the facts and phenomena connected with volcanic agency are brought within the comprehension of young minds.

Wonders of the Vegetable World. With Coloured Frontispiece and numerous Engravings. Royal 18mo. Price 1s.
A volume containing a large amount of interesting information regarding some of the more wonderful among the trees and plants of the world. The descriptions are clear and free from scientific technicalities, and each subject is further illustrated by well-executed pictures.

The Stars, including an Account of Nebulæ, Comets, and Meteors. With 50 Engravings. Royal 18mo. Price 1s. 6d.
A small volume containing a large amount of information, written with a view to serve as "a popular guide to a knowledge of the Stars and the Sidereal World." Scientific details are relieved by references to Greek mythology, and poetical quotations.

The Sun, Moon, and Planets. Their Physical Character, Appearance, and Phenomena. With 46 Engravings. Royal 18mo. 1s. 6d.
A companion volume to the preceding one, written and illustrated in the same style, regarding the wonders of our own solar system.

T. NELSON AND SONS, LONDON, EDINBURGH, AND NEW YORK.

Tales for the Young.

Alda's Leap, and Other Stories. By the Hon. Mrs. GREENE. Foolscap 8vo, cloth extra. 1s.

"The young reader will find a great deal to delight him. The stories are pretty and well told, and they deserve praise."—SCOTSMAN.

The Babe i' the Mill, and **Zanina the Flower-Girl of Florence.** By the Hon. Mrs. GREENE. Foolscap 8vo, cloth extra. 1s.

"The stories are strikingly original, and have peculiar quaintness and freshness of incident and dialogue."—DUBLIN MAIL.

The Adopted Brothers; or, Blessed are the Peacemakers. By M. E. CLEMENTS, Author of "The Story of the Beacon Fire," etc. Large foolscap 8vo, cloth extra. 1s.

A healthy story of two boys. How one by fostering jealousy in his heart brings much misery upon himself and unhappiness to his parents. A severe lesson clears away the mist, and the story ends in sunshine.

Annals of the Poor. Complete Edition, with Memoir of LEGH RICHMOND. Royal 18mo. 1s.

A cheap edition of these well-known Christian narratives, which so faithfully portray true piety in humble life.

The Babes in the Basket; or, Daph and Her Charge. By the Author of "Timid Lucy," etc. With Coloured Frontispiece and numerous Engravings. Royal 18mo. Price 1s.

The Basket of Flowers; or, Piety and Truth Triumphant. Illustrated. Royal 18mo. Price 1s.

A suitable story for a girl under twelve. It shows that right principles will sustain through greatest trials. Its incidents are interesting without being sensational.

The Giants, and how to Fight them. By the Rev. RICHARD NEWTON, D.D. With Coloured Frontispiece and numerous Engravings. Royal 18mo. 1s.

Dr. Newton possesses in the highest degree the art of interesting and instructing the young. The giants he here treats of are Selfishness, Ill-temper, Intemperance, and the like.

Godliness with Contentment is Great Gain. With Coloured Frontispiece. Royal 18mo. 1s.

A book for little boys and girls.

The Harrington Girls; or, Faith and Patience. By SOPHY WINTHROP. With Coloured Frontispiece. Royal 18mo. Price 1s.

On a very limited income three sisters manage to maintain a comfortable and cheerful home, and perform sundry charitable actions which meet with their due reward.

Hope On; or, The House that Jack Built. With Coloured Frontispiece and 25 Engravings. Royal 18mo. Price 1s.

The story of two orphans, forsaken and destitute in a great city: how God helped them, and how they helped others in the end.

The Story of the Lost Emerald; or, Overcome Evil with Good. By Mrs. EMMA MARSHALL, Author of "Over the Down," etc. Large foolscap 8vo, cloth extra. Price 1s.

A very interesting story hangs round this title. All who would hear of the valuable gem, of the various hands it passed through, and how it was alternately a curse and a blessing to its various possessors, should read this little volume.

T. NELSON AND SONS, LONDON, EDINBURGH, AND NEW YORK.

www.ingramcontent.com/pod-product-compliance
Lightning Source LLC
Chambersburg PA
CBHW031425230426
43668CB00007B/436